Stories of Don Quixote
Written Anew for Children

By James Baldwin

Table of Contents

Introduction

THE romance entitled "The Achievements of the Ingenious Gentleman, Don Quixote de la Mancha," was originally written in Spanish by Miguel de Cervantes Saavedra. It was published in two parts, the first in 1605 and the second in 1615—now just about three hundred years ago. Among the great books of the world it holds a permanent place. It has been translated into every language of Europe, even Turkish and Slavonic. It has been published in numberless editions. It has been read and enjoyed by men of the most diverse tastes and conditions.

The story is so simple that everyone can understand it, and yet it has in it so much wisdom that the wisest may derive pleasure from it. It touches the sense of humor in every heart. It moves to pity rather than ridicule, and to tears as well as laughter. And herein lies its chief claim to greatness, that it seems to have been written not for one country nor for one age alone, but to give delight to all mankind. "It is our joyfulest modern book."

In its original form, however, it is a bulky work, dismaying the present-day reader by its vastness. For it fills more than a thousand closely printed pages, and the story itself is interrupted and encumbered by episodes and tedious passages which are no longer interesting and which we have no time to read. The person who would get at the kernel of this famous book and know something of its plan and its literary worth, must either struggle through many pages of tiresome details and unnecessary digressions, or he must resort to much ingenious skipping. In these days of many books and hasty reading, it is scarcely possible that any person should read the whole of *Don Quixote* in its original form. And yet no scholar can afford to be ignorant of a work so famous and so enjoyable.

These considerations have led to the preparation of the present small volume. It is not so much an abridgment of the great book by Cervantes as it is a rewriting of some of its most interesting parts. While very much of the work has necessarily been omitted, the various adventures are so related as to form a continuous narrative; and in every way an effort is made to give a clear idea of the manner and content of the original. Although Cervantes certainly had no thought of writing a story for children, there are many passages in Don Quixote which appeal particularly to young readers; and it is hoped that this adaptation of such passages will serve a useful purpose in awakening a desire to become further acquainted with that great world's classic.

1. Getting Ready For Adventures

MANY years ago there lived in Spain a very old-fashioned gentleman whom you would have been glad to know. This gentleman had so many odd ways and did so many strange things that he not only amused his neighbors and distressed his friends, but made himself famous throughout the world.

What his real name was, no one outside of his village seemed to know. Some said it was this, some said it was that; but his neighbors called him "the good Mr. Quixana," and no doubt this was correct.

He was gentle and kind, and very brave; and all who knew him loved him. He had neither wife nor child. He lived with his niece in his own farmhouse close by a quiet little village in the province of La Mancha.

His niece was not yet twenty years of age. So the house was kept and managed by an old servant woman who was more wrinkled than wise and more talkative than handsome. A poor man who lived in a cottage nearby was employed to do the work on the farm; and he did so well that the master had much leisure time and was troubled but little with the cares of business.

Mr. Quixana was rather odd in his appearance and dress, as all old-fashioned gentlemen are apt to be.

He was more than fifty years of age, and quite tall and slender. His face was thin, his nose was long, his hair was turning gray.

He dressed very plainly. On week days he wore a coarse blouse and blue trousers of homespun stuff. On Sundays, however, he put on a plush coat and short velvet breeches and soft slippers with silver buckles.

In the hallway of his old-fashioned house a short, rusty sword was always hanging; and leaning against the wall were a rusty lance and a big rawhide shield. These weapons had belonged to his great-grandfather, long ago, when men knew but little about guns and gunpowder.

On the kitchen doorstep an old greyhound was always lying. This dog was very lean and slender, and his hunting days had long been past. But all old-fashioned gentlemen kept greyhounds in those days.

In the barn there was a horse as old and as lean as the greyhound. But of this horse I will tell you much more in the course of my story.

Like many other gentlemen, Mr. Quixana did not work much. He spent almost all his time in reading, reading, reading.

He was seldom seen without a book in his hand. When the weather was fine he would sit in his little library, or under the apple trees in his garden, and read all day.

He often forgot to come to his meals. He was so wrapped up in his books that he forgot his horse, his dog, and even his niece. He forgot his friends; he forgot himself. Sometimes he sat up and read all night.

Now, what kind of books do you suppose he read?

He read no histories nor books of travel. He cared nothing for poetry or philosophy. His whole mind was given to stories—stories of knights and their daring deeds.

He read so many of these stories that he could not think of anything else. His head was full of knights and knightly deeds, of magic and witchcraft, of tournaments and battlefields.

If he had read less, he would have been wiser; for much reading does not always improve the mind.

At length this old-fashioned gentleman said to himself, "Why should I always be a plain farmer and sit here at home? Why may I not become a famous knight?"

The more he thought about this matter the more he wished to be a hero like those of whom he had read in his books.

"Yes, I will be a knight," he said to himself. "My mind is fully made up. I will arm myself in a coat of mail, I will mount my noble steed, I will ride out into the world to seek adventures.

"No danger shall affright me. With my strong arm I will go forth to protect the weak and to befriend the friendless. Yes, I will be a knight, and I will fight against error wherever I find it."

So he began at once to get ready for his great undertaking.

The first thing to be done was to find some suitable armor. For what knight ever rode out into the world without being incased in steel?

In the garret of his house there was an old coat of mail. It had lain there among the dust and cobwebs for a hundred years and more. It was rusted and battered, and some of the parts were missing. It was a poor piece of work at the very best.

But he cleaned it as well as he could, and polished it with great care. He cut some pieces of pasteboard to supply the missing parts, and painted them to look like steel. When they were properly fitted, they answered very well, especially when no fighting was to be done.

With the coat of mail there was an old brass helmet. It, too, was broken, and the straps for holding it on were lost. But Mr. Quixana patched it up and found some green ribbons which served instead of straps. As he held it up and looked at it from every side, he felt very proud to think that his head would be adorned with so rare a piece of workmanship.

And now a steed must be provided; for every knight must needs have a noble horse.

9

The poor old creature in the barn was gaunt and thin and very bony; but he was just the stuff for a war horse, wiry and very stubborn. As the old-fashioned gentleman looked at him he fancied that no steed had ever been so beautiful or so swift.

"He will carry me most gallantly," he said, "and I shall be proud of him. But what shall I call him? A horse that is ridden by a noble knight must needs have an honorable and high-sounding name."

So he spent four days in studying what he should call his steed.

At last he said, "I have it. His name shall be Rozinante."

"And why do you give him that strange name?" asked the niece.

"I will tell you," he answered. "The word *rozin* means 'common horse,' and the word *ante* is good Latin for 'before' or 'formerly.' Now if I call my gallant steed 'Formerly-a-Common-Horse,' the meaning is plain; for everybody will understand that he is now no longer common, but very *uncommon*. Do you see? So his name shall be Rozinante."

Then he patted the horse lovingly, and gently repeated, "Rozinante! Rozinante!"

He thought that if he could only find as good a name for himself, he would feel like riding out and beginning his adventures at once. For what more could he need?

"Every knight," he said, "has the right to put Don at the beginning of his name; for that is a title of honor and respect. Now, I shall call myself Don— Don—Don something; but what shall it be?"

He studied this question for eight days. Then a happy thought came into his mind.

"I will call myself Don Quixote," he cried; "and since my home is in the district of La Mancha, I shall be known throughout the world as Don Quixote de la Mancha. What name is more noble than that? What title can be more honorable?"

The name was indeed not very different from his real name. For have we not said that his neighbors called him Quixana?

The good old gentleman had now mended and polished his armor and found new names for himself and his steed. He felt himself well equipped for adventures. But suddenly the thought came to him that still another thing must be settled before he could ride out and do battle as a real and true knight.

In all the stories he had read, every hero who was worthy of knighthood had claims to some fair lady whom he invoked in time of peril, and to whom he brought the prizes which he had won. It was at her feet that the knight must kneel at the end of every quest. It was from her that he must receive the victor's crown. To him, therefore, a lady friend was as necessary as a steed or a suit of armor.

Now Don Quixote was not acquainted with many ladies, but he felt that, as a knight, he must center his thoughts upon some one who would be his guiding star as he went faring through the world.

Who should it be?

This question troubled him more than any other had done. He sat in his house for two whole weeks, and thought of nothing else.

How would his niece do?

Well, she was very young, and he was her uncle. In all the books in his library there was no account of a knight kneeling at the feet of his own niece. She was not to be thought of.

As for his housekeeper, she was too old and homely. He could never think of doing homage to one in her humble station.

At length he remembered a handsome, red-cheeked maiden who lived in or near the village of Toboso. Her name was Adonza Lorenzo, and many years ago she had smiled at him as he was passing her on the road. He had not seen her since she had grown up, but she must now be the most charming of womankind.

He fancied that no lady in the world was better fitted to receive his knightly homage.

"Adonza Lorenzo it shall be!" he cried, rubbing his hands together.

But what a name! How would it sound when coupled with that of the valorous Don Quixote de la Mancha? Surely it was too common, and she must have a title more like that of a princess. What should it be?

He studied over this for many days, and at last hit upon a name which pleased him much.

"It shall be Dulcinea," he cried. "It shall be Dulcinea del Toboso. No other name is so sweet, so harmonious, so like the lady herself."

Thus, after weeks of labor and study, Don Quixote de la Mancha at length felt himself prepared to ride forth into the world to seek adventures. He waited only for a suitable opportunity to put his cherished plans into execution.

2. The Adventure at the Inn

ONE morning in midsummer, Don Quixote arose very early, long before anyone else was awake.

He put on his coat of mail and the old helmet which he had patched with pasteboard and green ribbons.

He took down the short sword that had been his great-grandfather's, and belted it to his side. He grasped his long lance. He swung the leather shield upon his shoulder.

Then he went out very quietly by the back door, lest he should awaken his niece or the housekeeper.

He went softly to the barn and saddled his steed. Then he mounted and rode silently away through the sleeping village and the quiet fields.

He was pleased to think how easily he had managed things. He was glad that he had gotten away from the house and the village without any unpleasant scenes.

"I trust that I shall presently meet with some worthy adventure," he said to himself.

But soon a dreadful thought came into his mind: He was not a knight, for no one had conferred that honor upon him; and the laws of chivalry would not permit him to contend in battle with anyone of noble rank until he himself was knighted.

"Whoa, Rozinante!" he said. "I must consider this matter."

He stopped underneath a tree, and thought and thought. Must he give up his enterprise and return home?

"No, that I shall never do!" he cried. "I will ride onward, and the first worthy man that I meet shall make me knight."

So he spoke cheeringly to Rozinante and resumed his journey. He dropped the reins loosely upon the horse's neck, and allowed him to stroll hither and thither as he pleased.

"It is thus," he said, "that knights ride out upon their quests. They go where fortune and their steeds may carry them."

Thus, leisurely, he sat in the saddle, while Rozinante wandered in unfrequented paths, cropped the green herbage by the roadside, or rested himself in the shade of some friendly tree. The hours passed, but neither man nor beast took note of time or distance.

"We shall have an adventure by and by," said Don Quixote softly to himself.

The sun was just sinking in the west when Rozinante, in quest of sweeter grass, carried his master to the summit of a gentle hill. There, in the valley below him, Don Quixote beheld a little inn nestling snugly by the roadside.

"Ha!" he cried. "Did I not say that we should have an adventure?"

He gathered up the reins; he took his long lance in his hand; he struck spurs into his loitering steed, and charged down the hill with the speed of a plow horse.

He imagined that the inn was a great castle with four towers and a deep moat and a drawbridge.

At some distance from the gate he checked his steed and waited. He expected to see a dwarf come out on the wall of the castle and sound a trumpet to give notice of the arrival of a strange knight; for it was always so in the books which he had read.

But nobody came. Don Quixote grew impatient. At length he urged Rozinante forward at a gentle pace, and was soon within hailing distance of the inn. Just then a swineherd, in a field nearby, blew his horn to call his pigs together.

"Ah, ha!" cried Don Quixote. "There is the dwarf at last. He is blowing his bugle to tell them that I am coming." And with the greatest joy in the world he rode onward to the door of the inn.

The innkeeper was both fat and jolly; and when he saw Don Quixote riding up, he went out to welcome him. He could not help laughing at the war-like appearance of his visitor—with his long lance, his battered shield, and his ancient coat of mail. But he kept as sober a face as possible and spoke very humbly.

"Sir Knight," he said, "will you honor me by alighting from your steed? I have no bed to offer you, but you shall have every other accommodation that you may ask."

Don Quixote still supposed that the inn was a castle; and he thought that the innkeeper must be the governor. So he answered in pompous tones:—

"Senior Castellano, anything is enough for me. I care for nothing but arms, and no bed is so sweet to me as the field of battle."

The innkeeper was much amused.

"You speak well, Sir Knight," he said. "Since your wants are so few, I can promise that you shall lack nothing. Alight, and enter!" And with that he went and held Don Quixote's stirrup while he dismounted.

The poor old man had eaten nothing all day. His armor was very heavy. He was stiff from riding so long. He could hardly stand on his feet. But with the innkeeper's help he was soon comfortably seated in the kitchen of the inn.

14

G·A·HARKER·

"I pray you, Senior Castellano," he said, "take good care of my steed. There is not a finer horse in the universe."

The innkeeper promised that the horse should lack nothing, and led him away to the stable.

When he returned to the kitchen he found Don Quixote pulling off his armor. He had relieved himself of the greater part of his coat of mail; but the helmet had

15

been tied fast with the green ribbons, as I have told you, and it could not be taken off without cutting them.

"Never shall anyone harm those ribbons," cried Don Quixote; and after vainly trying to untie them he was obliged to leave them as they were. It was a funny sight to see him sitting there with his head inclosed in the old patched-up helmet.

"Now, Sir Knight," said the innkeeper, "will you not deign to partake of a little food? It is quite past our supper time, and all our guests have eaten. But perhaps you will not object to taking a little refreshment alone."

"I will, indeed, take some with all my heart," answered Don Quixote. "I think I shall enjoy a few mouthfuls of food more than anything else in the world."

As ill luck would have it, it was Friday, and there was no meat in the house. There were only a few small pieces of salt fish in the pantry, and these had been picked over by the other guests.

"Will you try some of our fresh trout?" asked the landlord. "They are very small, but they are wholesome."

"Well," answered Don Quixote, "if there are, several of the small fry, I shall like them as well as a single large fish. But whatever you have, I pray you bring it quickly; for the heavy armor and the day's travel have given me a good appetite."

So a small table was set close by the door, for the sake of fresh air; and Don Quixote drew his chair up beside it.

Then the innkeeper brought some bits of the fish, ill-dressed and poorly cooked. The bread was as brown and moldy as Don Quixote's armor; and there was nothing to drink but cold water.

It was hard for the poor man to get the food to his mouth, for his helmet was much in his way. By using both hands, however, he managed to help himself. Then you would have laughed to see him eat; for, indeed, he was very hungry.

"No true knight will complain of that which is set before him," he said to himself.

Suddenly, however, the thought again came to him that he was not yet a knight. He stopped eating. The last poor morsel of fish was left untouched on the table before him. His appetite had left him.

"Alas! alas!" he groaned. "I cannot lawfully ride out on any adventure until I have been dubbed a knight. I must see to this business at once."

He arose and beckoned to the innkeeper to follow him to the barn.

"I have something to say to you," he whispered.

"Your steed, Sir Knight," said the innkeeper, "has already had his oats. I assure you he will be well taken care of."

"It is not of the steed that I wish to speak," answered Don Quixote; and he carefully shut the door behind them.

Then falling at the innkeeper's feet, he cried, "Sir, I shall never rise from this place till you have promised to grant the boon which I am about to beg of you."

The innkeeper did not know what to do. He tried to raise the poor man up, but he could not. At last he said, "I promise. Name the boon which you wish, and I will give it to you."

"Oh, noble sir," answered Don Quixote, "I knew you would not refuse me. The boon which I beg is this: Allow me to watch my armor in the chapel of your castle to-night, and then in the morning—oh, in the morning—"

"And what shall I do in the morning?" asked the innkeeper.

"Kind sir," he answered, "do this: Bestow on me the honor of knighthood. For I long to ride through every corner of the earth in quest of adventures; and this I cannot do until after I have been dubbed a knight."

The innkeeper smiled, and his eyes twinkled. For he was a right jolly fellow, and he saw that here was a chance for some merry sport.

"Certainly, certainly," he said, right kindly. "You are well worthy to be a knight, and I honor you for choosing so noble a calling. Arise, and I will do all that you ask of me."

"I thank you," said Don Quixote. "Now lead me to your chapel. I will watch my armor there, as many a true and worthy knight has done in the days of yore."

"I would gladly lead you thither," said the inn-keeper, but at the present time there is no chapel in my castle. It will do just as well, however, to watch your armor in some other convenient place. Many of the greatest knights have done this when there was no chapel to be found."

"Noble sir, I believe you are right," said Don Quixote. "I have read of their doing so. And since you have no chapel, I shall be content with any place."

"Then bring your armor into the courtyard of my castle," said the innkeeper. "Guard it bravely until morning, and at sunrise I will dub you a knight."

"I thank you, noble sir," said Don Quixote. "I will bring the armor at once."

"But stop!" cried the innkeeper. "Have you any money?"

"Not a penny," was the answer. "I have never read of any knight carrying money with him."

"Oh, well, you are mistaken there," said the innkeeper. "The books you have read may not say anything about it. But that is because the authors never thought it worthwhile to write about such common things as money and clean shirts and the like."

"Have you any proof of that?"

"Most certainly I have. I know quite well that every knight had his purse stuffed full of money. Everyone, also, carried some clean shirts and a small box of salve for the healing of wounds."

"It does look reasonable," agreed Don Quixote, "but I never thought of it."

"Then let me advise you as a father advises his son," said the innkeeper. "As soon as you have been made a knight, ride homeward and provide yourself with these necessary articles."

"I will obey you, most noble sir," answered Don Quixote.

He then made haste and got his armor together. He carried it to the barnyard and laid it in a horse trough by the well.

The evening was now well gone, and it was growing dark. Don Quixote took his shield upon his left arm. He grasped his long lance in his right hand. Then he began to pace to and fro across the barnyard. He held his head high, like a soldier on duty; and the old patched helmet, falling down over his face, gave him a droll if not fearful appearance.

The full moon rose, bright and clear. The barnyard was lighted up, almost as by day. The innkeeper and his guests stood at the windows of the inn, and watched to see what would happen.

Presently a mule driver came into the yard to water his mules. He saw something lying in the trough, and was stooping to take it out before drawing water from the well. But at that moment Don Quixote rushed upon him.

"Stop, rash knight!" he cried. "Touch not those arms. They are the arms of the bravest man that ever lived. Touch them not, or instant death shall be your doom."

The mule driver was a dull fellow and very slow. He but dimly understood what was said to him, and so paid no attention to the warning. He laid hold of the coat of mail and threw it upon the ground.

"O my lady Dulcinea! Help me in this first trial of my valor!" cried Don Quixote.

At the same moment he lifted his lance with both hands and gave the mule driver a thrust which laid him flat in the dust of the barnyard.

Another such knock would have put an end to the poor fellow. But Don Quixote was too brave to think of striking a fallen foe.

He picked up the coat of mail and laid it again in the horse trough. Then he went on, walking back and forth as though nothing had happened.

The poor mule driver lay senseless by the side of the trough. The innkeeper and his friends still watched from the inn.

"He is a hard-headed fellow," said one. "He is used to rough knocks, and will soon recover."

In a few minutes a noisy wagoner drove into the barnyard. He drove his team quite close to the trough. Then he began to clear it out in order to give water to his horses.

Don Quixote, however, was ready for him. He said not a word, but lifted his lance and hurled it at the wagoner's head. It is a wonder that the fellow's skull was not broken.

The wagoner fell to the ground, yelling most grievously. The people in the inn were frightened, and all ran quickly to the barnyard to put an end to the rough sport.

When Don Quixote saw them coming, he braced himself on his shield and drew his sword.

"O my Dulcinea, thou queen of beauty!" he cried. "Now give strength to my arm and courage to my beating heart."

He felt brave enough to fight all the wagoners and mule drivers in the world. But just then several of the wagoner's friends came running into the barnyard, and each began to throw stones at Don Quixote.

The stones fell in a shower about his head, and he was forced to shelter himself under his shield. Yet he stood bravely at his post, and nothing could make him abandon his arms.

"Fling on!" he cried. "Do your worst. I dare you to come within my reach."

He spoke with such fierceness that every man shrank back in fear. Some took refuge in the barn, but kept on throwing stones.

"Let him alone," cried the innkeeper. "He is a harmless fellow who wishes to become a knight. He has lost his senses through too much reading. Come away and leave him in peace."

The men stopped throwing stones. Don Quixote put down his shield and began again to pace back and forth between the horse trough and the barn. He allowed the servants to carry away the wounded wagoner and the unconscious mule driver; but he glared at them so fiercely that they were glad to get out of his reach.

The innkeeper began to think that he had carried the sport far enough. He was afraid that more and worse mischief might be done. So he spoke right gently to Don Quixote:—

"Brave sir, you have done nobly. You have guarded your armor with courage. You have shown yourself worthy of knighthood, and I will give you that honor without further delay."

"But it is not yet daybreak," answered Don Quixote. "I must guard my armor till the dawn appears."

"It is not at all necessary," said the innkeeper. "I have read of some very famous knights who stood guard only two hours; and you have watched for more than four hours although beset by many foes."

"Time flies swiftly when one is doing his duty," said Don Quixote. "The brave man is bravest when he curbs his anger; but if I am again attacked, I shall not be able to restrain my fury. Not a man in this castle shall be left alive unless it be to please you."

"You shall not be attacked," said the innkeeper. "You have guarded your armor quite long enough, and I will make you a knight at once, if you are willing."

"Nothing can please me better," answered Don Quixote; and he laid his lance gently down by the side of his armor.

The innkeeper, thereupon, called to his guests and servants to come and see the ceremony. A book was brought to him in which he kept his accounts of hay and straw. He opened it with much dignity while Don Quixote stood with closed eyes beside his armor.

The women of the inn gathered in a circle around them. A boy held a piece of lighted candle, while the innkeeper pretended to read a chapter from the book.

The reading being finished, Don Quixote knelt down in the dust of the barnyard. The innkeeper stood over him and mumbled some words without meaning. He gave him a blow on the neck with his hand. Then he slapped him on the back with the flat of his sword.

"Arise, Sir Knight," he said. "Thou are Don Quixote de la Mancha, the most valorous of men. Be brave, be brave, be always brave."

Don Quixote arose, feeling that he was now in truth a knight and ready to do valorous deeds.

One of the women handed him his sword. "May your worship be a lucky knight," she said.

Another arranged the green ribbons which held his helmet in place. "May you prosper, brave sir, wherever you go," she said.

21

Don Quixote threw his arms around the inn-keeper's neck and thanked him. He could not rest until he had done some gallant deed. So he sat up all the rest of the night, polishing his armor and thinking impatiently of the morrow.

3. The Adventure with the Farmer

AT the earliest break of day, Don Quixote made ready to ride out in quest of adventures. He buckled on his armor. He took his lance and his shield in his hands. His gallant steed, Rozinante, stood saddled and bridled at the door of the inn.

He again embraced the innkeeper. "Farewell, thou greatest of my benefactors," he cried. "May heaven bless thee for having made me a knight."

Then, with the help of a groom, he mounted and rode forth into the world.

Right gayly did he ride. For he felt that he was now in truth a knight, and his mind was filled with lofty thoughts.

Right gayly also did Rozinante canter along the highway, and proudly did he hold his head. For did he not know that he was carrying the bravest of brave men?

They had gone but a little way when Don Quixote suddenly remembered the innkeeper's command to provide himself with money, clean shirts, and some salve.

"The command must be obeyed," he said. "I must go home and get those necessary things."

So he turned his horse's head and took the first byroad that led towards his village. And now Rozinante seemed to have new life put into his lean body. He sniffed the air and trotted so fast that his heels seemed scarcely to touch the ground.

"This is after the manner of heroes," said Don Quixote. "Yet I still lack one thing. I need a faithful squire to ride with me and serve me. All the knights I have ever read about had squires who followed in their footsteps and looked on while they were fighting. I think, therefore, that while I am providing myself with money and shirts, I will also get me a squire."

Presently, as they were passing through a lonely place, the knight fancied that he heard distressing cries. They seemed to come from the midst of a woody thicket near the roadside.

"I thank Heaven for this lucky moment," he said to himself. "I shall now have an adventure. No doubt I shall rescue some one who is in peril, or I shall correct some grievous wrong."

He put spurs to Rozinante and rode as fast as he could to the spot from which the cries seemed to issue.

At the edge of the woody thicket he saw a horse tied to a small oak tree. Not far away, a lad of about fifteen years was tied to another oak. The lad's shoulders and back were bare, and it was he who was making the doleful outcry. For a stout country fellow was standing over him and beating him unmercifully with a horsewhip.

"Hold! hold!" cried Don Quixote, rushing up. "It is an unmanly act to strike a person who cannot strike back."

24

The farmer was frightened at the sudden appearance of a knight on horseback. He dropped his whip. He stood with open mouth and trembling hands, not knowing what to expect.

"Come, sir," said Don Quixote, sternly. "Take your lance, mount your horse, and we will settle this matter by a trial of arms."

The farmer answered him very humbly. "Sir Knight," he said, "this boy is my servant, and his business is to watch my sheep. But he is lazy and careless, and I have lost half of my flock through his neglect."

"What of that?" said Don Quixote. "You have no right to beat him, when you know he cannot beat you."

"I beat him only to make a better boy of him," answered the farmer. "He will tell you that I do it to cheat him out of his wages: but he tells lies even while I am correcting him."

25

"What! what!" cried Don Quixote. "Do you give him the lie right here before my face? I have a good mind to run you through the body with my lance. Untie the boy and pay him his money. Obey me this instant, and let me not hear one word of excuse from you."

The farmer, pale with fear, loosed the boy from the cords which bound him to the tree.

"Now, my young man," said Don Quixote, "how much does this fellow owe you?"

"He owes me nine months' wages at seven dollars a month," was the answer.

"Nine times seven are sixty-three," said the knight. "Sir, you owe this lad sixty-three dollars. If you wish to save your life pay it at once."

The farmer was now more alarmed than before. He fell upon his knees. He lifted his hands, imploring mercy. He sobbed with fright.

"Noble sir," he cried, "it is too much; for I have bought him three pairs of shoes at a dollar a pair; and twice when he was sick, I paid the doctor a dollar."

"That may be," answered Don Quixote, "but we will set those dollars against the beating you have given him without cause. Come, pay him the whole amount."

"I would gladly do so," said the farmer, "but I have not a penny in my pocket. If you will let the lad go home with me, I will pay him every dollar."

"Go home with him!" cried the lad. "Not I. Why, he would beat me to death and not pay me at all."

"He won't dare to do it," answered Don Quixote. "I have commanded him and he must obey. His money is at his house. I give him leave to go and get it. His honor as a knight will make him pay his debt to you."

"A knight!" said the lad. "He is no knight. He is only John Haldudo, the farmer."

"What of that?" said Don Quixote. "Why may not the Haldudos have a knight in the family?"

"Well, he is not much of a knight. A knight would pay his debts," said the lad.

"And he will pay you, for I have commanded him," said Don Quixote.

Then turning to the farmer, he said, "Go, and make sure that you obey me. I will come this way again soon, and if you have failed, I will punish you. I will find you out, even though you hide yourself as close as a lizard."

The farmer arose from his knees and was about to speak, but the knight would not listen.

"I will have no words from you," he said. "You have naught to do but to obey. And if you would ask who it is that commands you, know that I am the valorous

Don Quixote de la Mancha, the righter of wrongs and the friend of the downtrodden. So, good-by!"

Having said this, he gave spurs to Rozinante and galloped away.

The farmer watched him until he was quite out of sight. Then he turned and called to the boy.

"Come, Andrew," he said. "Come to me now, and I will pay thee what I owe thee. I will obey this friend of the downtrodden."

"You will do well to obey him," said the boy. "He is a knight, and if you fail to pay me, he will come back and make things hot for you."

"Yes, I know," answered the farmer. "I will pay you well and show you how much I love you."

Then, without another word, he caught hold of the boy and again tied him to the tree. The boy yelled lustily, but Don Quixote was too far away to hear his cries. The farmer fell upon him and beat him with fists and sticks until he was almost dead. Finally he loosed him and let him go.

"Now, Andrew, find your friend of the downtrodden," he said. "Tell him how well I have paid you."

Poor Andrew said nothing. He hobbled slowly away, while the farmer mounted his horse and rode grimly homeward.

In the meanwhile, Don Quixote was speeding toward his own village. He was very much pleased with himself and with his first adventure as a knight.

"O Dulcinea, most beautiful of beauties," he cried, "well mayest thyself be happy. For thy knight has done a noble deed this day."

And thus he rode gallantly onward, his lance clanging against his coat of mail at every motion of his steed.

4. The Adventure with the Merchants

DON QUIXOTE had not ridden more than two miles when, at a turn in the road, he saw several horsemen approaching him.

G·A·HARKER

They were merchants of Toledo, and they were going to some distant town to buy silks. There were six of them, and each carried an umbrella over his head to shield him from the sun.

Following behind these horsemen there were four servants and three mule drivers, all on foot.

Don Quixote's heart beat fast when he saw this company.

"Here is an adventure worthy of my courage!" he cried.

He fixed himself in his stirrups, he couched his lance, he covered his breast with his shield. Then he posted himself in the middle of the road at the top of a gentle hill.

As soon as the merchants were within hearing, he cried out, "Halt there! Let all mankind stand still. No person shall pass here unless he is ready to declare that the peerless Dulcinea del Toboso is the most beautiful lady in the universe."

The merchants stopped in wonder at the strange being who thus barred their way. They were not long in guessing the truth.

"It is some poor gentleman who has lost his senses," they said to one another.

Then their leader rode forward a few paces and saluted the knight.

"Sir Knight," he said, "we do not know the fair lady whom you name. If you will let us see her, and if she proves to be as beautiful as you think, we will agree to all that you require of us."

"Let you see her!" cried Don Quixote. "I might do that if I chose. But the importance of the thing is in making you confess and declare her beauty without seeing her.

Come now, raise your right hands and say what I demand of you.

The merchants sat quietly in their saddles, and made no answer.

"What!" cried Don Quixote. "Are you silent? Then know that I am your enemy, and I challenge you to combat right here and now."

He braced himself in his saddle and shook his lance; but still the merchants made no reply.

"Are you afraid, you cowards?" shouted the knight. "Come one by one; or come all together, as you please. I am ready for the combat."

Then he spurred his horse and rode furiously down the hill towards the astonished merchants.

There is no telling what might have happened had Rozinante behaved himself. But that gallant steed had gone scarcely twenty yards when he stumbled and fell in the middle of the road.

Don Quixote was pitched headlong into the dust. His long lance went flying into the weeds on one side of the highway; his shield was thrown among the bushes on the other. The knight himself made a funny appearance as he rolled and tumbled on the ground. The weight of his rusty armor held him down.

But even while he lay helpless in the dust, he was a hero with his tongue. "Stay, you cowards!" he shouted. "Do not run away. It is my horse's fault that I have been thus dismounted."

The merchants laughed. His sorry plight amused them no less than his wonderful pluck. They spread their umbrellas above their heads and rode onward over the hill.

But one of the mule drivers, who was an ill-natured fellow, could not bear to hear his master called a coward. He picked up the fallen lance and broke it in pieces. Then with one of the longer parts he belabored Don Quixote's sides until it was splintered into a dozen fragments. Nor did he stop until he was quite tired out.

Still Don Quixote was not conquered. Through all this storm of blows he lay kicking on the ground and daring his enemies to do their worst. "Slay me if you will," he cried, "but, still I affirm that the Lady Dulcinea is without her equal on earth."

At last the mule driver left him and ran onward to overtake his mules and his master.

When Don Quixote found himself alone he tried once more to get on his feet. But if he was unable to do this at first, how was he to do it now, all bruised and battered as he was?

As he lay helpless on his back it so happened that a plowman came that way. This plowman, who lived in Don Quixote's village, had been to the mill and was returning with a bag of meal on his donkey's back.

When he saw the knight sprawling in the dust he stopped, while the donkey began to make acquaintance with poor Rozinante who was picking grass by the roadside.

"Hello, my good friend!" cried the plowman. "What has happened to you?"

Don Quixote did not answer. He looked up at the sky and began to repeat a long speech he had read in one of his books.

"The fellow has lost his senses," said the plowman to himself.

Then he stooped and lifted the knight's helmet from his face. It was the helmet that had been patched with pasteboard and tied on with green ribbons; but the mule driver had broken it with kicks and blows, and the ribbons were torn into shreds.

As soon as the plowman saw the knight's face he knew him.

"Oh, my good neighbor Quixana," he said, "how came you here, and what is the matter?"

The poor gentleman paid no attention to his friend, but kept on repeating passages from his books. In fact, he was very badly hurt.

The plowman, with a good deal of trouble, lifted him up and set him astride of the donkey. He placed him so that he could lean over and rest upon the bag of meal. Then he got all the knight's armor together, and even the splinters of the lance, and tied them on the back of Rozinante.

Having seen that everything was secure, he took the steed by the bridle and the donkey by the halter, and, walking before them, he made his way slowly toward the village. He trudged thoughtfully along, often looking back and speaking kindly to the wounded man; but Don Quixote, resting on the bag of meal, answered only with sighs and groans. He complained most dolefully, but would not tell how he had fallen into misfortune.

"My dear Quixana," at length said the plowman, "I fear you do not know me."

"That is no matter," said Don Quixote. "I know very well who I am. What's more, I am perhaps not only myself but a dozen other brave knights all joined in one."

It was about sunset when they reached the village. The plowman did not wish his neighbors to see the poor knight in his battered and bruised condition, for he

31

knew that much depended upon keeping him as quiet as possible. So he tarried in a grove outside of the village until daylight had faded into dusk.

Then he led the poor man to his own house.

As he went up cautiously to the door he heard voices within.

The curate of the village and his friend the barber were there. These men were neighbors of Don Quixote, and it had been their habit to come in often and spend a pleasant evening with him.

The plowman stopped at the door and listened.

"What do you think?" cried the housekeeper. "My master has not been seen for two whole days. His horse, his shield, his lance, and the old armor that was his grandfather's have also disappeared."

"Indeed! And where can he have gone?" inquired the curate.

"Where? Where but riding over the world and making believe that he is a knight!" answered the woman. "It's all because of those vile books which he was forever poring over."

The niece then spoke. "Certainly it's the books," she said. "The books made him foolish. Why, I have known him to read forty-eight hours without stopping. Then he would fling the book from him and make believe draw his sword, slashing it about him in a most fearful manner."

"I have known him to do even wilder things than that," said the housekeeper. "Once, in broad daylight, he ran around this very room shouting that he had killed four giants as tall as church steeples. It was the books. They made him mad."

"Indeed, that's true," declared the niece. "It was the books—and they ought to be burned every one of them."

"You are right," said the curate. "Those books have unsettled his mind. Before the setting of another sun they shall be brought to trial and condemned to the flames."

During all this discourse the plowman and Don Quixote were just outside of the door, unseen, in the darkening twilight. Now, without more ado, the plowman cried out,

"Hello there, house! Open the gates, for here are a dozen valorous knights who bring a prisoner with them."

The housekeeper shrieked and dropped her broom on the floor. The curate and the barber rushed to the door, and the niece followed them with the lighted candle in her hand. When they saw Don Quixote astride of the donkey they all ran to embrace him.

"Have a care," he groaned. "Be gentle, for I am sorely hurt. It was all on account of my steed failing me. Carry me to bed, and send for the enchantress, Urganda, to heal my wounds."

"There! Didn't I say so?" whispered the housekeeper to the curate. "His head is full of those wicked books."

"Where are you wounded, uncle?" asked the niece.

"Wounded! I'm not wounded. I'm only bruised. I had a bad fall from Rozinante while I was fighting ten giants. You never saw such giants. They were the wickedest fellows that ever roamed the earth; but I was a match for them."

"Hear him!" whispered the curate to the housekeeper. "He talks of giants. It is as we feared. Those vile books must be condemned and burned without further delay."

They lifted the knight from the donkey's back. They helped him into the house and put him in his favorite chair.

Then the women asked him a thousand questions; but his only answer was that they should give him something to eat and let him alone.

This they did.

When he had eaten a hearty supper he crept off to bed without so much as saying good-night.

33

5. The Library

EARLY the next morning the curate and the barber came again. Don Quixote was still sleeping. Indeed, he did not awake until the day was more than half gone.

"We have come to remove the cause of his illness," said the curate; and he asked the niece to give him the key to the room where her uncle kept his books.

"Here it is," she said; "and I hope you will make clean work of it."

They unlocked the door and went in, the housekeeper following them. There, ranged neatly on shelves, they saw a hundred large volumes and a goodly number of smaller ones. The curate began to read the titles.

"Wait! wait!" cried the housekeeper. She ran out and soon came back with a sprinkling can full of water.

"Here, doctor," she said, "take this and sprinkle every nook and corner of the room. Some unseen sorcerer may be lurking among the books, and the water will drive him out."

The curate smiled and did as she desired. Then he asked the barber to hand him the books one by one, while he opened them and examined the title-pages.

"They are not all equally bad," he said. "Perhaps there are some that do not deserve to be burned."

"Oh, no!" cried the niece. "Do not spare any of them. Everyone is bad. Everyone has helped to undo my uncle."

"Throw them out of the window into the garden," said the housekeeper. "Then we will carry them around into the back yard and burn them where the smoke will not annoy anybody."

They worked all the morning. Often the curate would find a volume over which he would linger for some time. He would turn the leaves lovingly and look slyly at the pictures.

"It is a great pity to burn that," he would whisper; and then he would lay the book aside for his own reading.

The most of the volumes, however, were romances of knighthood and of really no value. The quick eye of the curate easily detected such trash as these, and they were cast out and doomed to destruction.

Towards noon everyone began to tire of the business. "It's no use to examine any more of these volumes," said the curate. "They're all bad. Cast them out! Cast them out!"

The housekeeper was delighted. A bonfire was kindled in the back yard, and, while the curate and the barber were resting themselves, she threw into it not only the books which had been condemned but also the pleasant volumes which the good curate had decided to spare for his own edification.

Thus the good sometimes perish with the bad.

In the afternoon Don Quixote awoke from his long sleep. He was so bruised and so lame, however, that he could not rise. He could only lie in bed and feebly mutter the names of the housekeeper and his niece.

They brought him some food, and when he had eaten it he fell asleep again.

"It is best to let him rest," whispered the curate; and they left him alone.

For two whole days the knight did not go out of his room. But he was well cared for, and though he suffered not a little, he was never heard to complain.

While he thus lay helpless in his bed, the curate and the barber paid frequent visits to the house. They spent much time in stopping up the door of the little room where the knight's library had been. This they did so cunningly that the housekeeper herself could not tell exactly where the door had been.

"If he cannot find the room, he will soon forget about the books," said the curate.

On the fourth day, Don Quixote was able to walk about a little; but he did not seem to feel sure of himself or of any object about him.

The first thing he did was to look for his library.

He went feebly up and down the long hallway, trying to find the door. He felt of the wall. He groped here and there, and stared confusedly around him. At length he gave up the search; but he said not a word to anyone.

The next day he spoke to the housekeeper, "I do believe that I have lost the way to the study."

"What study?" asked the woman. "There is no study in this house."

"I feel quite sure that I once had a study with many books in it," said Don Quixote.

"Oh, that was long ago," answered the housekeeper. "But during your sickness one of those wicked enchanters, about whom you have read, ran away with it. He took not only the room but all the books that were in it."

Don Quixote groaned.

"Yes, uncle," said the niece, "an enchanter did it. He came one night, riding on a dragon. He alighted and went into your study. In a little while, he flew out through the chimney. He left the house so full of smoke that we could not see our own eyes. We looked everywhere for your library, but could find neither room nor books."

"I think I know who it was," said Don Quixote. "It was that famous enchanter, Freston. He has a spite against me and is my worst enemy."

"You are right, uncle," said the niece. "It was either Freston or Friston. At any rate his name ended with *t-o-n*."

"He is a bad fellow," answered the knight. "No doubt he will try to do me some other mischief. He knows where I live and will come often. But I am not afraid of him. Someday I will meet him in fair fight and vanquish him."

Then he arose and with his feeble hands took down the sword which had been hanging over the mantelpiece ever since his sad return. He felt of its edge, and murmured,

"Ah, Freston, Freston! Thou shalt yet learn of the prowess of the valorous Don Quixote de la Mancha!"

6. The Choosing of a Squire

FOR fifteen days the good old gentleman stayed at home. He moved quietly about the house, and seemed happy and contented. The loss of his library did not disturb him.

"A true knight will bear the disappointments of life with becoming fortitude," he said.

The niece and the housekeeper, and indeed everyone else, began to hope that he would forget his strange delusion. They spoke to him cheerfully and tried to keep his mind on other things.

The curate called to see him every day, and they had many pleasant talks on many pleasant subjects. But always towards the end, Don Quixote would ramble back to the thoughts which still seemed uppermost in his memory.

"I tell you what, my dear friend," he would say, "the world would be better off if there were more knights in it. What we need most is knights, knights, plenty of knights."

Then he would go on for an hour or more talking upon his favorite subject. The good curate would nod his head and smile. He knew that it was better to humor his poor friend and let him have his own way.

As the days passed by, Don Quixote became more and more uneasy. The house was too quiet for him. He longed to be riding forth in quest of new adventures. He could not think or talk of anything else.

"But there is one thing lacking," said he to the curate. "I must find me a squire. All the knights that I ever read about had faithful squires who followed them on their journeys and looked on while they were fighting."

The curate smiled and said nothing.

Now there lived in the village a poor man whose name was Sancho Panza. He was a common laborer who had often done odd jobs about Don Quixote's farm. He was honest but poor—poor in purse and poor in brains.

To this man Don Quixote had taken a strange fancy. Almost every day he walked down the street to talk with him. He was just the kind of fellow he wished for his squire.

At last he mentioned the matter. "Sancho Panza," he said, "I am a knight and I shall soon ride out on a knightly errand. You cannot do better than to go with me as my squire. I promise that you shall earn great renown, second only to myself."

"Renown, good master?" queried Sancho; "and what sort of a thing is that?"

"Why, your name will be in everybody's mouth," answered Don Quixote. "All the great ladies and gentlemen will be talking about your achievements."

"How very fine that will be!" said Sancho.

"And it may happen that in one of my adventures I shall conquer an island," continued Don Quixote. "Indeed, it is very likely that I shall conquer an island. Then, if you are with me, I will give it to you to be its governor."

39

"Well, I don't know much about islands," said Sancho, "but I'm sure I should like to govern one. So, if you'll promise me the first island you get, I'll be your man. I'll go with you and do as you say."

"I promise," said Don Quixote. "You shall be my squire; and since you will share my labors, you shall also share my rewards."

Then followed busy days for Don Quixote. He provided himself with money by selling a part of his farm. He mended his broken armor. He borrowed a lance of a friendly neighbor. He patched up his old helmet as best he could.

At last everything was in readiness, and the knight went down the street to talk with Sancho Panza. He wished to advise him of the hour he expected to start.

"I will be ready, sir," said Sancho.

"And be sure you have with you whatever it is necessary to carry," said Don Quixote. "Above all things, bring your wallet."

"Indeed I will, master," said Sancho; "and I will also bring my dappled donkey along. For I am not much used to foot travel."

Don Quixote was puzzled. He could not remember of reading about any knight whose squire rode on a donkey. Yet he feared to offend Sancho, lest he should lose his services, which now seemed indispensable to him.

"Your dappled donkey? Oh, certainly!" he said. "You may ride him until good fortune shall present you with a horse. And I promise that the first discourteous knight who meets us shall give up his steed to you."

"I thank you, master," said Sancho Panza; "but being used to the donkey, I shall be more at home on his back than on the back of any prancing steed you might give me."

7. The Adventure with the Windmills

VERY early the next morning, the knight and his squire set out on their travels. They stole silently away from the village without bidding good-by to anyone; and they made such haste that at sunrise they felt themselves quite safe from pursuit.

Don Quixote, riding in full armor astride of gaunt Rozinante, felt that he was indeed the most valorous knight in the world; and no doubt he was a formidable sight. As for Sancho Panza, he rode like a patriarch, with his knapsack on one side of him and a leather bottle on the other, his feet almost dragging on the ground. His mind was full of thoughts about that island of which he hoped to be the governor.

The sun rose high above the hills. The two travelers jogged onward across the plains of Montiel. Both were silent, for both had high purposes in view.

At length Sancho Panza spoke: "I beseech you, Sir Knight-errant, be sure to remember the island you promised me. I dare say I shall make out to govern it, let it be ever so big."

Don Quixote answered with becoming dignity: "Friend Sancho, you must know that it has always been the custom of knights-errant to conquer islands and put their squires over them as governors. Now it is my intention to keep up that good custom."

"You are indeed a rare master," said Sancho Panza.

"Well, I am thinking I might even improve upon that good custom," said Don Quixote. "What if I should conquer three or four islands and set you up as master of them all?"

"You could do nothing that would please me better," answered Sancho.

While they were thus riding and talking, they came to a place where there were a great many windmills. There seemed to be thirty or forty of them scattered here and there upon the plain; and when the wind blew, their long white arms seemed to wave and beckon in a droll and most threatening manner.

Don Quixote drew rein and paused in the middle of the road.

"There! there!" he cried. "Fortune is with us. Look yonder, Sancho! I see at least thirty huge giants, and I intend to fight all of them. When I have overcome and slain them we will enrich ourselves with their spoils."

"What giants?" asked Sancho Panza.

"Why, those who are standing in the fields just before us," answered the knight. "See their long arms! I have read that some of their race had arms which reached more than two miles."

"Look at them better, master," said Sancho. "Those are not giants; they are windmills. The things which you call arms are sails, and they flap around when the wind blows."

"Friend Sancho," said the knight, very sternly, "it is plain that you are not used to adventures. I tell you those things are giants. If you are afraid, go and hide yourself and say your prayers. I shall attack them at once."

Without another word he spurred Rozinante into a sturdy trot and was soon right in the midst of the windmills.

"Stand, cowards!" he cried. "Stand your ground! Do not fly from a single knight who dares you all to meet him in fair fight."

At that moment the wind began to blow briskly and all the mill sails were set moving. They seemed to be answering his challenge.

He paused a moment. "O my Dulcinea, fairest of ladies," he cried, "help me in this perilous adventure!"

Then he couched his lance; he covered himself with his shield; he rushed with Rozinante's utmost speed upon the nearest windmill.

The long lance struck into one of the whirling sails and was carried upward with such swiftness that it was torn from the knight's firm grasp. It was whirled into the air and broken into shivers. At the same moment the knight and his steed were hurled forward and thrown rolling upon the ground.

G·A·HARKER-

Sancho Panza hurried to the place as quickly as his dappled donkey could carry him. His master was lying helpless by the roadside. The helmet had fallen from his head, and the shield had been hurled to the farther side of the hedge.

"Mercy on me, master!" cried the squire. "Didn't I tell you they were windmills?"

44

"Peace, friend Sancho," answered Don Quixote, rubbing the dust from his eyes. "There is nothing so uncertain as war. That wicked enchanter, Freston, who stole my books has done all this. They were giants, as I told you; but he changed them into windmills so that I should not have the honor of victory. But mind you, Sancho, I will get even with him in the end."

"So be it, say I!" cried Sancho, as he dismounted from his donkey.

He lifted the fallen knight from the ground. He brought his shield and adjusted his helmet. Then he led his unlucky steed to his side and helped him to remount.

The sun was now sloping towards the west, and knight and squire rode thoughtfully onward across the plain of Montiel.

8. The Adventure with the Monks

THROUGH all that afternoon Don Quixote and his squire jogged slowly along, and neither house nor other friendly shelter did they see. The sun had gone down, and twilight was darkening when they saw near the road a clump of green trees which seemed to offer them a safe resting place.

"Here, Sancho," said the knight, "let us go no farther. Since there is no castle nor even an inn in this barren country we must lodge here in this grove."

They dismounted, and while Sancho was caring for the animals Don Quixote strolled around among the trees.

On an old oak he found a withered branch some ten feet long and quite smooth and straight. With much labor he wrenched it from the tree; he carried it back to his lodging place and began with much patience to remove the twigs from it.

"This will serve me instead of the lance which I lost in my encounter with the windmill," he said. "I have read of knights who used such makeshifts and did wonderful deeds with them."

Night came on. He sat silently upon the bare ground and looked at the stars. His mind was full of the stories he had read of heroes in forests and in deserts keeping guard through the hours of darkness. And so he sat bravely awake until the morning dawned.

As for Sancho Panza, he did not spend the night in that foolish fashion. He sprawled himself upon a bed of leaves, closed his eyes, and made one nap of it. Had not his master wakened him he would have slept till high noon.

They lost no time in breakfasting. To the valorous Don Quixote the day held so many promises that he was unwilling to waste a moment. They saddled their steeds, they mounted, and were away with the rising of the sun.

After many miles of travel they came at length to a more rugged country; and in the afternoon they entered the pass of Lapice where the road runs through a narrow valley between rocky hills.

"Here, Sancho," said Don Quixote, "here is the place where we may have our fill of adventures."

"Do you think that you will find me that island somewhere near?" asked Sancho Panza.

"Indeed, I cannot say," answered his master. "But I wish to caution you on a very particular point. It is I that am to do the fighting. You may see me in great danger and beset by many foes; but you must not offer to fight for me unless you know that those foes are only common scoundrels. The laws of chivalry forbid a squire to encounter a knight."

"I see, I see," said Sancho, "and I shall do as you say. For I was never any great hand at fighting, and I don't get into quarrels with anyone if I can help it."

"For a man in your humble station, that is right," said Don Quixote.

"Still, if a knight should set upon me first," said Sancho, "I am not sure but that I would give him a few hard whacks."

"That would be right and I will not forbid it," said Don Quixote. "But as for helping me against any knight or knights, I command you not to do it."

"I'll obey you. I'll obey you, master," said Sancho. "I have no desire to encounter any knight or knights."

While they were thus talking they saw two monks riding leisurely down the pass towards them. The monks were dressed in black robes and mounted on mules so high and stately as to look like travelers on the backs of camels. They wore masks over their faces to keep off the dust; and each held an umbrella above him as a shield from the sun.

A little way behind the monks there came a four-wheeled coach drawn by two small horses. Following this were four or five mounted men and two mule drivers on foot.

Inside of the coach sat a richly dressed lady who was traveling to the nearest city.

"I think we are about to have a famous adventure," said Don Quixote.

"Why so?" asked Sancho.

"Well, I am quite sure that those two persons in black are magicians who are carrying away some princesses in that coach. It is my duty to prevent so wicked an act."

"Ah!" sighed Sancho, "I'm afraid this will be a worse affair than the windmills."

The next moment Don Quixote gave spur to his steed and galloped forward in the middle of the road to meet the approaching monks.

"Halt there, you lawless magicians!" he cried. "I command you to give those high-born princesses their freedom, or else prepare for instant death."

The monks stopped their mules and lifted their masks. They wondered what sort of man this was whom they had met; for indeed he made a strange appearance.

"Sir Knight," they cried, "we are not magicians. We are religious men, going about our own affairs. We know nothing about any princesses."

"You cannot deceive me," answered Don Quixote. "I know you well enough, and none of your enchantments will prevail against me."

Then, without further parley, he couched his lance, set spurs to his steed, and dashed furiously upon the nearest monk.

The monk, taken by surprise, flung himself to the ground on the farther side of his mule. In this way he saved his life; for, had Don Quixote struck him with the rude lance from the oak tree, he would certainly have been killed.

The other monk was badly frightened. He lashed his mule's flanks and fled out of the pass and over the plain as though racing with the wind.

By this time Sancho Panza had come up. He slipped quickly from his donkey's back, and ran up to the first monk, who was still on the ground, and began to strip him of his robe.

"Why do you do that, you robber?" cried the two mule drivers, who were, in fact, the servants of the monks.

"I am not a robber," answered Sancho. "I'm only taking the spoils which my master has lawfully won in battle."

But the rude fellows cared nothing for his words. They fell upon him and beat him without mercy. They threw him into a ditch by the roadside. They stamped upon him, and left him sprawling in the mud without sense or motion.

The monk, seeing that Don Quixote had ridden onward, now climbed upon his mule as quickly as possible. With whip and spur he urged the poor beast forward and went speeding away after his friend. He neither paused nor looked behind until he was safely out of the pass.

In the meanwhile Don Quixote had halted the coach and dismounted beside it. He looked in at the door and began to address the lady.

"Fair Princess," he said, "I am the valorous knight, Don Quixote de la Mancha. I have given battle to your captors and am pleased to say that you are now delivered from their power. I ask no recompense for my valorous deed; but I beg that you go on to Toboso and there tell my Lady Dulcinea of the great service I have rendered to you."

At that moment one of the lady's squires came riding up in haste. He seized the stick which Don Quixote called his lance, and wrenched it from his hands.

"Get gone!" he cried in bad Spanish. "Leave the coach or I'll kill thee as sure as I am a Biscayan."

"Were you a gentleman, as you are not, I would chastise you as you deserve," said Don Quixote.

"What!" cried the Biscayan. "Me no gentleman? I'll show thee that I'm a gentleman—a gentleman by land, a gentleman by sea, a gentleman in spite of everything."

"Then, if you are a gentleman, I will try titles with you," said Don Quixote.

With that he remounted with surprising quickness and, sword in hand, dashed furiously upon the Biscayan.

The fellow was so taken by surprise that, had not his unruly mule reared and leaped to one side, he might have fared badly in the encounter. But, quickly recovering himself, he snatched a cushion from the coach to serve as a shield, and with his other hand drew his sword.

50

The lady screamed. Her coachman, cracking his whip, drove away at a rattling speed. The road was left clear for the desperate combat.

With swords raised in air, Don Quixote and the Biscayan faced about and glared fiercely at each other. The foot servants and mule drivers, who now came running forward, tried in vain to pacify them. Don Quixote would not so much as look at them.

"O Dulcinea, thou flower of beauty," he cried, "lend help to me, thy champion in this most dangerous encounter."

At the next moment, the Biscayan's sword fell with a mighty blow upon his back. Had not his armor been of such rare good metal, his body would have been cleft in halves. Luckily, however, no harm was done, save to the edge of the Biscayan's weapon.

Don Quixote steadied himself, recovering from the blow. He gripped his sword with a firmer grasp; he raised it high in the air; he gathered all his strength for the final stroke.

The servants and mule drivers who saw him were terrified by his rage. The lady in the coach, who was now looking back from a safe distance, clasped her hands and vowed to the saints to do all sorts of good deeds, if only her squire might escape from his deadly peril.

But why should I prolong this chapter to describe the result of that ever memorable conflict? Here you may see the Biscayan struggling with his unruly mule, covering himself with his cushion, and swinging his battered sword in the air. And here you may behold the valorous Don Quixote de la Mancha, with uplifted blade, urging his steed to the conflict, and—

But let us draw the curtain and end the chapter without another word.

9. The Lost Helmet

DOUBTLESS you have already guessed how the great combat between Don Quixote and the Biscayan ended.

As the knight rushed blindly forward, his enemy's sword descended for the second time. Had it not turned in his hand the story of Don Quixote would be ended here. Luckily, however, it did no further damage than to destroy the knight's helmet and shave off half of his left ear.

Before Don Quixote could return the blow the Biscayan's mule became unmanageable. It leaped suddenly forward and ran with great speed into the open plain. It ran straight for the lady's coach; but in vaulting over a brook it twisted its body so suddenly as to hurl its master to the ground.

The poor Biscayan was stunned by the fall. He lay helpless and senseless in the mud and mire.

Don Quixote was not far behind. He checked his steed when in full gallop, and slipped nimbly from the saddle. He ran to his fallen foe and set the point of his sword against his breast.

"Now yield thee as a recreant, or thy head shall pay the forfeit!" he cried.

The Biscayan scarcely heard him, but lay speechless at his feet. There is no telling what might have happened had not the lady leaped from the coach and ran to the rescue. With tears she besought Don Quixote to spare the life of her faithful squire.

"Truly, most beautiful lady," said the victorious knight, "I will grant your request. I will spare his life on one condition."

"What is the condition?" asked the lady.

"He must give me his word of honor," answered Don Quixote, "that he will go straightway to Toboso. At Toboso he must present himself, in my name, to the peerless lady Dulcinea. She will dispose of him as she thinks best."

"I promise it for him," said the lady. "He will do all that you require of him."

"Then he may live," said Don Quixote.

He bowed gallantly to the lady. He remounted his steed. He turned himself about with great dignity, and resumed his journey as though nothing had happened.

Sancho Panza was not long in overtaking his master. He rode up to him and seized his hand.

"If it please you, my good Don Quixote," he said, "don't forget to make me governor of the island you have won in this great fight."

"Brother Sancho," answered Don Quixote, "these are not adventures of islands. These are only little skirmishes along the road. We can expect from them nothing more than broken heads and bleeding ears. But have patience, have patience! Perhaps in the next adventure I shall conquer a kingdom."

"How nice that would be!" said Sancho. "But does not your ear give you pain?"

"It is only a trifle," answered Don Quixote. "No true knight ever complains of trifles."

"But he permits his wounds to be dressed. Come! I have some lint and a little white salve in my wallet."

They paused beneath a spreading tree, and while Sancho was binding up the bleeding ear, his master kept on talking.

"Friend Sancho," he asked, "did you ever read in history of any knight who showed more skill, or greater activity than I did in this memorable combat?"

"No, never," answered Sancho. "I can safely say that I never, in any book of history, read of any knight so active as you. For you must know that I never learned to read nor even to write."

"Be very gentle, friend Sancho," said Don Quixote, wincing under his rough surgery. "The boldest knight has feelings after the battle has been won."

"Never did I serve a bolder knight than you, good master," answered Sancho, "and your ear is now very gently dressed."

Don Quixote put up his hand to touch the injured part, and as he did so he discovered for the first time the loss of his helmet.

"Tell me, Sancho, where is my helmet?" he cried.

"I think you lost it on the field of battle," answered the squire.

Don Quixote forgot the dignity that belongs to knighthood. He could scarcely be made to believe that his helmet was not still on his head. Then he began to rave. You would have thought him stark, staring mad.

But in a few minutes he became more calm. With his right hand on his sword, he lifted his eyes towards the tree tops and made a solemn vow.

"Never, while I live," said he, "will I eat bread on a tablecloth till I have taken revenge on the knight who has done me this injury."

"Dear master," said Sancho, "think on what you are saying. If the fellow who split your helmet has gone on to Toboso, according to promise, to deliver himself to the lady Dulcinea are you not already even with him?"

"It may be as you say," answered Don Quixote. "I will, therefore, change the wording of my vow and declare that never, so long as I live, will I eat bread on a tablecloth till I have captured another helmet as good as the one that I have lost."

"So far, so good," said Sancho. "But suppose we should not for a long time meet anyone with a helmet on. Think of the sad case we shall be in. There are few who travel this road except wagoners and mule drivers, and they never wear helmets."

"You are mistaken," answered Don Quixote. "Before we go much farther we shall see more men at arms than you ever dreamed of."

Sancho Panza made no reply. He remounted his donkey, and the two rode onward through the pass of Lapice. As they rode they beguiled the time with much talk concerning knighthood and other matters no less lofty and inspiring.

They journeyed slowly through the hill country beyond the pass. At night they rested in a friendly inn, and the next day and for many days they jogged aimlessly along, ready for any new adventures.

And adventures they had in great plenty—perilous adventures, amusing adventures, chivalrous adventures; but of all the persons whom they met, there was not one who wore a helmet. Don Quixote was therefore obliged to ride bareheaded and to eat bread from uncovered tables.

56

10. The Adventure with the Sheep

ONE day as they passed the crest of a hill, they saw a great cloud of dust rising in the road at some distance below them. Don Quixote's eyes flashed with excitement as he watched it.

"The day has come, Sancho," he cried; "the day has come that shall bring us good fortune and happiness. Now I shall perform an exploit that will be remembered through the ages. See'st thou that cloud of dust, Sancho?"

"I see it, brave master," answered the squire.

"Well, that dust is raised by an army that is marching this way," said Don Quixote. "It is a mighty army made up of many nations."

"If that is the case," said Sancho, "there must be two armies. For, over to the left of us, there is another cloud of dust."

Don Quixote looked, and his heart was filled with joy; for he firmly believed that two vast armies were marching towards each other and about to meet in battle. His mind was so filled with fights, adventures, enchantments, and other wonderful things which he had read about, that his fancy easily changed everything he saw into something that he wished to see.

Even his own eyes could not make him believe that the dust was raised by two large flocks of sheep which were being driven along the road. He was so positive about the two armies that even Sancho soon began to feel that he was right.

"Well, sir, what are we to do now?" asked the squire.

"Our duty is plain," answered the knight. "What ought we to do but aid the weaker and injured side? The army in front of us is commanded by the great Alifanfaron, emperor of the vast island of India. The army on our left is led by his enemy, King Pentapolin of the naked arm."

"Pray tell me, brave master," said Sancho, "what is the cause of the trouble? Why are those two great men going thus together by the ears?"

"It is the old, old story," answered Don Quixote. "Alifanfaron is a Pagan, and he is in love with Pentapolin's daughter, who is a Christian. But he shall not have her unless he becomes converted and gives up his false belief."

"No, never!" cried Sancho. "I will stand by Pentapolin and his daughter, and help them all I can."

"You are right," said Don Quixote. "There is no need of being a knight to fight in such battles. Men of all conditions may take part in this conflict."

Then pointing to the clouds of dust with his long finger, he described the various warriors whom he imagined were marching to the conflict. Sancho Panza listened in silence. He turned his eyes this way and that, trying to see the knights and valiant men whom his master was naming.

At last, growing impatient, he cried, "You might as well tell me it is snowing; for not a man nor knight can I see either in this cloud of dust or that."

"Indeed!" answered Don Quixote, "but don't you hear their horses neigh, their trumpets sound, their drums beat?"

"Not I," said Sancho. "I open my ears very wide, and I hear nothing but the bleating of sheep."

And now the two flocks were drawing very near to them, and the sheep could not only be heard, but plainly seen.

"You are frightened, Sancho," said Don Quixote. "Go hide yourself in some safe place while I alone charge into the ranks of the heathen."

Then he couched his lance, set spurs to Rozinante, and rushed onward like a thunderbolt to meet the nearest flock.

Sancho Panza looked after him in amazement. "Hold, sir!" he cried. "Come back! Are you mad? Those are sheep, and neither pagans nor Christians. Come back, I say."

But Don Quixote did not hear him. He rode forward furiously. "Courage, brave knights!" he shouted. "March up, fall on, the victory is ours! Follow me, and take your revenge!"

He charged into the midst of the flock. He thrust right and left, and began to spear the poor dumb creatures as gallantly as though they were his mortal enemies.

The men who were driving the sheep called out to him, but he would not listen. He rushed madly this way and that. The sheep were routed and trampled upon in a most terrible manner.

"Where is the general of this army?" cried Don Quixote. "Where art thou, proud Alifanfaron? See, here is a single knight who challenges thee to combat, and who will punish thee for this unjust war." The shepherds were now greatly alarmed. They ran forward and began to throw stones at the knight. Some of these, as big as a man's fist, flew close about his ears; some fell upon his shield; and others belabored the back and sides of unhappy Rozinante. But, paying no attention to this shower of missiles, Don Quixote rode unafraid, shouting as though in the thick of battle, and seeking everywhere for some worthy foe.

"Where art thou, Alifanfaron?" he cried again. But just at that moment a stone struck him in the side with such force as almost to break his ribs.

He reeled in his saddle. He felt sure that he was killed, or at least badly wounded. But he remembered the bottle of healing balsam which the innkeeper had advised him to carry, and he felt in his pocket for it.

He was about to put the bottle to his lips, when—bang! Another stone came whizzing through the air. It broke the bottle; it maimed his hand; it struck him fairly on the mouth.

Such a blow was too much for the valiant knight to withstand. He fell from his horse and lay upon the ground as though dead.

The shepherds got their flocks together and hurried away with all speed. They feared that they had killed the knight and that greater trouble would follow.

Throughout the strange conflict, Sancho sat on his dappled donkey at the top of the hill. He felt ashamed and alarmed at sight of his master's mad doings. He groaned, and tore his beard in vexation and dismay.

But when he saw the knight knocked from his steed and stretched upon the ground, he hastened to his aid.

"Ah, master," he cried, "this comes of not taking my advice. Did I not tell you that it was a flock of sheep and no army?"

Don Quixote groaned and sat up.

"Friend Sancho," he said, "it is an easy matter for enchanters to change the shapes of things as they please. At the very moment that my victory was complete my old enemy changed the routed army into a flock of sheep. It was all done to rob me of the glory that belonged to me."

"Well, I saw nothing but sheep from the first," said Sancho.

Don Quixote, with much ado, arose and stood on his feet. He opened his mouth and felt of the teeth that had been loosened by that last cruel blow.

"Friend Sancho, learn of me," he said. "All these storms are only the signs of calmer days. Better success will soon follow. Neither good luck nor bad luck will last always."

"At any rate," interrupted Sancho, "many words will not fill a bushel. I think you would make a better preacher than knight-errant."

"Knights-errant," answered Don Quixote, "ought to know everything. Some of them have been as good preachers as any who preach in the churches."

"Very well," said Sancho. "You may have it as you will. But let us leave this unlucky place and seek lodgings where we may rest and have a bite of wholesome food."

He helped his master to climb again upon the back of gentle Rozinante, and then he remounted his dappled donkey.

"My trusty Sancho, go thy own pace," said Don Quixote. "I will follow thee."

Sancho obeyed, and led the way, keeping to the road which passed over the hills. Don Quixote followed him, riding slowly and gently; for he had been so bruised and wounded in his encounter with the shepherds, that every movement of his steed gave him pain.

11. The Adventure with the Barber

DAYS passed, and still Don Quixote rode bare-headed: for as yet he had found no means whereby to win for himself a new helmet. Every day, however, had its adventures, and every turn of the road seemed to lead the knight and his squire into new fields of action.

One morning as they were riding along a highway from a small village to a larger one, they saw a horseman coming slowly towards them.

"See there!" cried Don Quixote. "Now I shall have an adventure that will redound to my glory."

"Why do you think so?" asked Sancho.

"Do you not see that horseman?" answered Don Quixote. "He wears something on his head that glitters like gold. If I mistake not, he is a knight, and it is Mambrino's helmet that he wears."

"Mambrino's helmet, master!" said Sancho. "What about Mambrino's helmet?"

"Thou knowest my vow, Sancho," was the answer. "To-morrow I shall eat bread on a tablecloth. For that knight who is riding toward us on his prancing steed has a helmet of gold on his head."

"I don't see any knight," said Sancho. "I see only a common man riding a gray donkey much like my own. There is something bright on the top of his head; but all is not gold that glitters."

"I tell thee, it is Mambrino's helmet, and it is gold!" cried Don Quixote, growing angry.

Now the truth of the matter is this: The smaller of the two villages I have mentioned had no barber. The people, therefore, were obliged to depend on the barber of the larger village, who rode over whenever he was wanted.

Sometimes he was called upon to trim the men's beards, sometimes to dress the ladies' hair; but he was oftenest required to bleed some person who was not feeling well. For in those times it was the custom, when anyone was sick, to open one of his veins and let the "bad" blood run. This was thought to be the best medicine and a cure for all sorts of ailments.

To do this bloodletting was, indeed, the main business of a barber. His sign was a pole with red stripes running spirally around it. These red stripes represented the bloody bandage which was used to bind up the wound. The same sign is used by barbers even now; but good barbers never bleed their customers.

G·A·HARKER

In those olden times, the barber always had a brass basin in which to catch the blood as it flowed from the patient's arm. This basin was kept very bright and clean; for it was a necessary thing in every barber's shop, and often used.

And now let us go back to our story. The "knight on his prancing steed" was nobody but the barber of the bigger village, riding on his gray donkey to visit his patients in the smaller village.

The morning was cloudy, and rain might begin to fall at any minute. The barber had a new hat which the rain would spoil. To guard against this misfortune, he clapped his brass basin, upside down, upon his head. It covered hat and all, and was proof against the rain.

Don Quixote, as we know, wanted a helmet. He had read so much about Mambrino's helmet that he could think of nothing else. His mind, having dwelt so long upon this subject, could turn anything he chose into a golden helmet. Some people in our own times can do as much.

As the barber came nearer, the knight raised his lance, which you will remember was only the branch of a tree. He braced himself in his stirrups and made ready for a charge.

Then he shouted, "Wretch, defend thyself, or at once surrender that which is justly mine." And without further parley, he rushed upon the barber as fast as Rozinante, with his blundering feet, could carry him.

The barber saw him coming, and had just time enough to throw himself from his donkey and take to his heels. He leaped the hedge at the side of the road and ran across the fields with the swiftness of a deer. But the brass basin, having slipped from his head, was left lying in the dust.

Don Quixote checked his steed. "Here, Sancho!" he cried. "Here is my helmet. Come and pick it up."

"Upon my word, that is a fine basin," said Sancho, as he stooped and handed it to his master.

Don Quixote, with great delight, clapped it on his head. He turned it this way and that, and tilted it backward and forward.

"It is pretty large," he said. "The head for which it was made must have been a big one. The worst is, that it has no visor, and half of one side is lacking."

Sancho could not help smiling.

"What is the fool grinning at now?" cried his master, angrily.

"Oh, nothing," answered Sancho. "I was only thinking what a big jolthead it must have been to wear a helmet so much like a barber's basin."

"Well, it does look like a barber's basin," said Don Quixote. "But that is because some enchanter has changed its form. When we come to a town where there is an armorer, I will have it made over into its proper shape; for there is no doubt that it is really the helmet of the famous Mambrino."

He turned it about on his head, and pulled it well down over his ears.

"I'll wear it as it is," he said. "It is better than nothing."

"There is that knight's dappled steed," said Sancho, pointing to the barber's gray donkey which was nibbling grass by the roadside. "I have a good mind to exchange my own faithful beast for him."

"Well, exchange is no robbery," answered Don Quixote. "We do not plunder those whom we meet, for that would be unbecoming to a knight. The dappled steed is no doubt very dear to its master and therefore should be spared to him; but I give thee leave, Sancho, to exchange saddles."

"You are a wise master," said Sancho; and without another word he made his own poor donkey look three times better by dressing him in the barber's saddle.

Then, well satisfied with themselves and their plunder, the knight and the squire renewed their journey.

12. The Adventure with the Prisoners

DAY after day, the two travelers jogged slowly along, rambling hither and thither wherever their fancy chose to wander. At length they came into the rugged highway which leads through the Black Mountains, or, as they are called in Spain, the Sierra Morena.

"Now we shall have our fill of adventures," said Don Quixote.

It was to be even so; for at the top of the first hill they saw twelve strange men trudging along the highway and slowly approaching them. The men were all in a row, one behind another, like beads on a string; for they were linked to a long chain by means of iron collars around their necks.

In front of this procession rode two horsemen with guns; and the rear was brought up by two foot guards with swords and clubs.

"See there, master," said Sancho. "See those poor fellows who are being taken away to serve the king in the galleys."

"Why are they being treated in that ugly fashion?" asked Don Quixote, reining in his steed.

"Well, they are rogues," was the answer. "They have broken the law and been caught at it. They are now on their way to the king's galleys to be punished."

"If that is the case," said Don Quixote, "they shall have my help. For I am sworn to hinder violence and oppression."

"But these wicked wretches are not oppressed," said Sancho. "They are only getting what they deserve."

Don Quixote was not satisfied. "At any rate, they are in trouble," he answered.

Soon the chain of prisoners had come up.

"Pray, sir," said Don Quixote to one of the mounted men who was captain of the guards, "why are these people led along in that manner?"

"They are criminals," answered the captain. "They have been condemned to serve the king in his galleys. I have no more to say to you."

"Well, I should like to know what each one has done," said Don Quixote.

"I can't talk with you," said the captain. "But while they rest here at the top of the hill, you may ask the rogues themselves, if you wish. They are so honest and truthful that they will not be ashamed to tell you."

Don Quixote was much pleased. He rode up to the chain and began to question the men.

"Why were you condemned to the galleys, my good fellow?" he asked of the leader.

"Oh, only for being in love," was the careless answer.

"Indeed!" cried Don Quixote. "If all who are in love must be sent to the galleys, what will become of us?"

"True enough!" said the prisoner. "But my love was not of the common kind. I was so in love with a basket of clothes that I took it in my arms and carried it home. I was accused of stealing it, and here I am."

Don Quixote then turned to another. "And what have you done, my honest man?" he asked. "Why are you in this sad case?"

"I will tell you," answered the man. "I am here for the lack of two gold pieces to pay an honest debt."

"Well, well, that is too bad," said the knight. "I will give you four gold pieces and set you free."

"Thank you, sir," said the prisoner. "But you might as well give money to a starving man at sea where there is nothing to buy. If I had had the gold pieces before my trial, I might now be in a different place."

Thus Don Quixote went from one prisoner to another, asking each to tell his history.

The last man in the chain was a clever, well-built fellow about thirty years old. He squinted with one eye, and had a wickeder look than any of the others.

Don Quixote noticed that this man was strangely loaded with irons. He had two collars around his neck, and his wrists were so fastened to an iron bar that he could not lift his hands to his mouth.

The knight turned to one of the foot guards. "Why is this man so hampered with irons?" he asked.

"Because he is the worst of the lot," was the answer. "He is so bold and cunning that no jail nor fetters will hold him. You see how heavily ironed he is, and yet we are never sure that we have him."

"But what has he done?" asked Don Quixote.

"Done!" said the guard. "What has he not done? Why, sir, he is the famous thief and robber, Gines de Passamonte."

Then the prisoner himself spoke up quickly. "Sir, if you have anything to give us, give it quickly and ride on. I won't answer any of your questions."

"My friend," said Don Quixote, "you appear to be a man of consequence, and I should like to know your history."

"It is all written down in black and white," answered Gines. "You may buy it and read it."

"He tells you the truth," said the guard. "He has written his whole history in a book."

"What is the title of the book?" asked Don Quixote. "I must have it."

"It is called the *Life of Gines de Passamonte*, and every word of it is true," answered the prisoner. "There is no fanciful tale that compares with it for tricks and adventures."

"You are an extraordinary man," said Don Quixote.

By this time the guards had given the command and the human chain was again toiling slowly along over the hill. But Don Quixote was not yet satisfied. He followed, making a long speech first to the prisoners and then to the guards. At length he raised himself in his stirrups, and cried out:—

"Gentlemen of the guard, I am the renowned Don Quixote de la Mancha. I command you to release these poor men. If you refuse, then know that this lance, this sword, and this invincible arm will force you to yield."

"That's a good joke," said the captain of the guard. "Now set your basin right on top of your empty head, and go about your business. Don't meddle any more with us, for those who play with cats are likely to be scratched."

This made Don Quixote very angry. "You're a cat and a rat, and a coward to boot!" he cried. And he charged upon him so suddenly and furiously that the captain had no time to defend himself, but was tumbled headlong and helpless into the mud.

The other guards hurried to the rescue. They attacked Don Quixote with their swords and clubs, and he, wheeling Rozinante around, defended himself with his heavy lance. He would have fared very badly had not the prisoners made a great hurly-burly and begun to break their chain.

Seeing the confusion and wishing to give aid to his master, Sancho leaped from his donkey, and, running up to Gines de Passamonte, began to unfasten his irons. The conflict which now followed was dreadful. The guards had enough to do to defend themselves from the wild thrusts of Don Quixote's lance. They seemed to lose their senses, so great was the uproar.

The prisoners soon freed themselves from their irons and were masters of the field. The guards were routed. They fled with all speed down the highway, followed by a shower of stones from the prisoners. It was a mile to the nearest village, and thither they hastened for help.

Sancho Panza remounted his donkey and drew up to his master's side. "Hearken," he whispered. "The king's officers will soon be after us. Let us hurry into the forest and hide ourselves."

"Hush," said Don Quixote, impatiently. "I know what I have to do."

Then he called the prisoners around him and made a little speech:—

"Gentlemen, you understand what a great service I have rendered you. For this I desire no recompense. But I shall require each one of you to go straightway to the city of Toboso and present himself before that fairest of all ladies, the matchless Lady Dulcinea. Give her an exact account of this famous achievement, and receive her permission to seek your various fortunes in such ways and places as you most desire."

The prisoners grinned insolently, and Gines de Passamonte made answer:—

"Most noble deliverers, that which you require of us is impossible. We must part right quickly. Some of us must skulk one way, some another. We must lie hidden in holes and among the rocks. The man hounds will soon be on our tracks, and we dare not show ourselves. As to going to Toboso to see that Lady Dulcinea, it's all nonsense."

These words put Don Quixote into a great rage. He shook his lance at the robber, and cried out:—

"Now you, Sir Gines, or whatever be your name, hear me! You, yourself, shall go alone to Toboso, like a dog with a scalded tail. You shall go with the whole chain wrapped about your shoulders, and shall deliver the message as I have commanded."

Gines smiled at this bold threat, and made no answer. But his companions with one accord fell upon the knight, dragged him from his steed, and threw him upon the ground.

They stripped him of his coat and even robbed him of his long black stockings. One of them snatched the basin from his head and knocked it against a rock until it was dinted and scarred most shamefully. And one broke his long lance in two and threw it into a thicket of thorns.

As for Sancho, he fared but little better. They took his coat, but left him his vest. They would have taken his shoes had they been worth the trouble.

Having thus amused themselves for a few hasty minutes, the rascals departed. They scattered in different directions, each one to shift for himself. They were much more anxious to escape the officers of the law than to present themselves before the Lady Dulcinea del Toboso.

Thus the dappled donkey, Rozinante, Sancho Panza, and Don Quixote were left the sole masters of the field. But they were sorry masters, every one of them.

"Friend Sancho," said Don Quixote, rising from the muddy road, "there is a proverb which I desire thee to remember. It is this: One might as well throw water into the sea as do a kindness to clowns."

He sought in the thicket for his broken lance, and, having recovered the half of it, he made shift to climb upon Rozinante's back. The day was far gone, and he rode silently and thoughtfully onward into the heart of the Black Mountains. And Sancho Panza, on his dappled donkey, followed him.

13. In the Black Mountains

THE darkness of night found our two travelers in the midst of the mountains and far from any friendly inn. The sky was clear, however, and above the tree tops the round, full moon was shining brightly. Both knight and squire were weary from long traveling, and sore from the beating which they had received from the ungrateful thieves.

"Here we are!" at length cried Sancho, pulling up his donkey by the side of a huge rock. "Here we are, master. This is a pleasant, sheltered place. Let us tarry here till morning."

"Truly, I am willing," said Don Quixote.

Both men were so tired that they were loath to get down from their steeds. They sat quietly in their saddles, thinking, thinking; and soon both were fast asleep.

Don Quixote sat upright, bracing himself with the remnant of his oaten lance which he had rescued from the thicket. Sancho doubled himself over upon the pommel of his saddle, and snored as peacefully as though he were on a feather bed. As for Rozinante and patient Dapple, they were no less weary than their masters. They stood motionless in their places, and nothing short of a goad could have caused them to stir.

It chanced about midnight that the thief, Gines de Passamonte, came to this very spot, seeking the best way to escape from the forest. As he was passing by the great rock, he was astonished to see the two beasts and their riders resting quietly in its shadow. He crept up to them very gently, not wishing to disturb their slumbers.

"Ha!" he whispered to himself, "how soundly they sleep! These two foolish fellows ride safely along the public road, and are afraid of nothing. But I, with all my smartness, am obliged to skulk through the woods and tire myself to death with much walking. I wish I had one of these steeds."

He walked around Rozinante and gently felt of his ribs and stroked his long head. "He is only a frame of bones," he said, "and there's no telling how soon he may fall to pieces. I might manage to ride him, but at the end of the road I could neither sell him nor give him away."

Then he went softly up to the dappled donkey and examined him from his nose to his hoofs.

"This beast could carry me, I know; and I could sell him for a dollar or two anywhere. But how shall I get him?"

He leaned against the rock and thought the matter over, while Sancho Panza made the woods resound with his snoring.

"It would be easy enough to tumble him off and take his steed by main force," said Gines, still talking to himself. "But the poor fellow did me a good turn to-day, and I don't like to disturb his slumbers."

Presently he took his jackknife from his pocket and went stealthily into a grove of small trees by the roadside. There, having found some slender saplings, he cut four strong poles as large as his wrist and as long as his body.

With these in his hands he returned to the donkey and slyly unbuckled the girths of the saddle. Sancho Panza, with his feet firmly in the stirrups and his short body doubled snugly upon the pommel, was not at all disturbed. He snored so loudly that no other sound could possibly be heard.

The cunning Gines smiled at his own ingenuity. He placed one end of each of his four poles under a corner of the saddle, the other end resting firmly upon the ground. Then he carefully and very gradually moved the bottom ends closer and closer to the donkey's feet. This, of course, raised the saddle some inches above the animal's back, while Sancho still slept the sleep of the weary.

Gines tried each pole to see that it stood like a brace, strong and secure. Then he led the donkey out from under, leaving the saddle and Sancho high up in the air.

It was a funny sight, there in the still light of the moon; and Gines de Passamonte looked back and laughed. He then threw himself upon the donkey's bare back and rode joyfully away.

Sancho Panza slept and snored, and stirred not an inch. The hours of the night passed silently by, and the moon and stars journeyed slowly down the western sky. At length the day dawned, and the sunlight began to peep through the trees.

Sancho was at most times an early riser. With the coming of the morning he stopped snoring. Then he slowly opened his eyes, raised his arms, and yawned. The motion of his body caused the supporting poles to twist around and give way; the saddle suddenly turned beneath him, and he fell sprawling to the ground.

The sudden noise awoke Don Quixote.

"Where is thy donkey, friend Sancho?" he asked, looking quickly around.

"You may well ask where is my donkey," answered the squire, rising from the ground and rubbing his eyes. "My donkey's gone. Some thief has led him away in the night, and left me nothing but four sticks and the saddle which I got in exchange from the barber."

"Thief, indeed!" said Don Quixote. "It was no thief. Those same wicked enchanters have done it. They have changed the poor beast into four sticks; and now you will have to walk until we learn how to remove the enchantment and change the sticks back to a donkey."

Sancho Panza was sorely distressed. He looked at the saddle and at the sticks, and then at the tracks which the donkey had left in the dust of the road. Tears came to his eyes, and he broke out into the saddest and most pitiful lamentation that ever was heard.

"Oh, my Dapple, my donkey! Oh, dear one, born and bred under my own roof! Thou wert the playfellow of my children, the comfort of my wife, the envy of my neighbors. Thou wert the easer of my burdens, the staff and stay of my

75

life. And now, thou art gone, thou art gone. Oh, my Dapple, my donkey! How can I live without thee?"

Don Quixote's kind heart was touched. "Never mind, dear Sancho," he said. "Dry thy tears. I have five donkeys at home, and I will give thee an order on my niece for three of them. I will write it with the first pen and ink we encounter."

This generous offer turned Sancho's grief into joy. It dried his tears; it hushed his cries; it changed his moans to smiles and thanks.

"You were always a good master," he said; "and I would rather meet with that pen and ink than with any number of knights."

Then knight and squire sat down together on the ground and munched some bits of dry bread merely to say they had breakfasted. And after Rozinante had eaten his fill of the sweet grass by the roadside, they resumed their journey through the mountains. Don Quixote rode in advance, and Sancho followed slowly with the donkey's saddle astride of his shoulders.

14. The Message to Dulcinea

ONE day as Don Quixote with his squire was strolling aimlessly through the roughest and wildest part of the mountains, he became suddenly very silent. "Friend Sancho," he said, "as you value your life, I bid you not to speak a word to me until I give you leave."

His mind was filled with queer, unreasoning fancies, and he seemed to be pondering upon some new and weighty subject.

So, all the day, they toiled wearily and slowly along, and neither spoke to the other.

Sancho Panza was very tired. He was almost ready to burst for want of a little chat. Still, with the saddle on his shoulders, he trudged silently at the heels of Rozinante, and kept his thoughts to himself.

At length, however, he could bear it no longer. He quickened his pace till he came alongside of his master. Then he laid his hand on Don Quixote's knee, and spoke:—

"Good sir, give me your blessing and let me go home to my wife and children. There I may talk till I am weary, and nobody can hinder me. I tell you, this tramping over hills and dales, by night and by day, without opening my lips, is killing me. I cannot endure it."

"Friend Sancho, I understand thee," answered Don Quixote, "and I give thee leave to use thy tongue freely so long as we are alone together on this mountain road."

"Then let us make hay while the sun shines," cried Sancho. "I will talk while I can, for who knows what I may do afterward. Every man for himself, and God for us all, say I. Little said is soonest mended. There is no padlocking of men's mouths; for a closed mouth catches no flies."

"Pray have done with your proverbs," said Don Quixote, sternly. "Listen to me, and I will unfold a plan which I have formed for my future course and for yours also, dear Sancho."

Then he explained to the squire that it was his intention to send him forthwith to Toboso to carry a letter to the Lady Dulcinea.

"I desire that you shall start within three days," he said, "and as you are very poor at walking, you may have the use of Rozinante, who will carry you with great safety and speed."

"Very well, master," said Sancho; "but what will you do while I am gone?"

"Do? Do you ask what I will do?" answered the knight. "Why, I have a mind to imitate that famous knight, Orlando, I mean to go mad, just as he did. I will throw away my armor, tear my clothes, pull up trees by the roots, knock my head against rocks, and do a thousand other things of that kind. You must wait and see me in some of my performances, Sancho, and then you must tell the Lady Dulcinea what you have beheld with your own eyes."

"Oh, you need not go to any trouble about it," said Sancho; "for I will tell the lady just the same. I will tell her of your thousand mad tricks, and bring you back her answer all full of sweet words."

"As for those tricks, as you call them," said Don Quixote, "I mean to perform them seriously and solemnly, for a knight must tell no lies. But I will write the letter immediately, and you shall set out on your journey to-morrow at sunrise."

"And please, sir," said Sancho, "do not forget to write that order to your niece for those three donkeys which you promised me."

They stopped in the midst of a green thicket of underwoods, and there, after much ado, the letter was written and also the order for the donkeys. These were scrawled with a bit of charcoal in a little notebook which Don Quixote happened to find in his pocket.

"They are not very plainly written, Sancho," he said; "but, in the first village to which you come, it will be easy to have the schoolmaster copy them neatly for you."

Sancho took the notebook and put it carefully in his waistcoat pocket. "Now I am even wild to be gone," he said. "I will mount Rozinante, and be off at once; for a bearer of messages should never delay his starting. Give me your blessing, dear master, and I will not wait to see any of your tricks."

"Nay," said Don Quixote. "Wait a little while, for you should see me practice twenty or thirty mad gambols, such as knocking my head against rocks, and the like. I can finish them in half an hour."

"Say not so," answered Sancho. "It would grieve me to the heart to see you playing the madman. I would cry my eyes out; and I have already blubbered too much since I lost my poor donkey. But I will tell the Lady Dulcinea about your tricks, just the same as though I had seen you do them."

"Then I will give thee my blessing and let thee go," said Don Quixote.

"But tell me, good master," said Sancho, "what will you do for food when I am gone? Will you rob travelers on the highway, and steal your dinner from the shepherds hereabout?"

"Don't worry about that, Sancho," said his master. "I shall feed on the herbs and fruits of the forest, and want nothing more; for it is the duty of a mad knight to half starve himself. But you shall find me in good condition when you return."

"But now another thing comes into my head," said Sancho. "How shall I know this out-of-the-way place when I come back? How shall I find you again in this wilderness?"

"Strew a few green branches in the path, Sancho. Strew them as you ride along till you reach the main highway. They will serve as a clew to show you the way hither, if by chance you should forget the turning place."

"I will go about it at once," said Sancho.

So he went among the trees and cut a bundle of green boughs. Then he came and asked his master's blessing; and after both had wept many tears, he mounted Rozinante.

"Be good to the noble steed, Sancho," said Don Quixote. "Remember to be as kind to him as you have been to his master."

"Indeed, I will not forget," said Sancho; and he rode away, strewing the boughs as he went.

Don Quixote watched him until a turn of the road hid him from sight. Then he wandered into the wildest part of the woods, and was really as mad as the maddest knight he had ever read about.

15. Sancho Panza on the Road

THE next day as Sancho Panza was plodding slowly along the highway, he came to a little inn. He knew the place quite well, for he and his master had lodged there not a month before.

It was dinner time, and the odors of the kitchen filled the air. Sancho's mouth watered at the thought of a bit of hot roast beef; for he had tasted nothing but cold victuals for many days.

He rode up to the gate and stopped. He had had some trouble with the servants on his former visit to this inn, and therefore he had some misgivings about the reception that might now be given him. So he sat still, outside the gate, and enjoyed the savory smells which came to him through the open windows.

Presently, two men came out, and when they saw him at the gate, they paused. Then one said to the other,—

"Look there, master doctor, isn't that Sancho Panza?"

"Most surely it is," said the other; "and more than that, he rides Don Quixote's horse."

Now these two men were the curate and the barber of Don Quixote's own village. They were the men who had passed sentence on his books, and they knew more than anyone else about the poor man's malady.

They were now going through the country in search of him; for they wished to persuade him to return to the care of his family and friends.

They spoke to Sancho, and he was not a little surprised to meet them in that out-of-the-way place.

"Where is your master, Sancho? Where is Don Quixote?" they asked.

"My master is engaged with some important business of his own," answered Sancho, quite stiffly.

"But where is he?" said the curate.

"That I dare not tell you," said Sancho.

"Now, Sancho Panza!" cried the barber, "don't try to put us off with any flimflam story. If you don't tell us where he is, we shall believe you have murdered him and stolen his horse. So, out with it. Tell us the truth, or we'll have you laid by the heels and punished as you deserve."

"Oh, come now, neighbors!" said Sancho. "Why should you threaten me? I don't know where my master is at this particular moment; but I left him in yonder mountain, knocking his head against the trees, tearing up rocks, and doing a thousand queer things which I need not mention."

Then he told the whole story as I have told it to you, adding to it a great many fanciful touches of his own.

"And now," he said, "I am on my humble way to Toboso, where I mean to give my master's letter into the hands of the Lady Dulcinea."

"Let us see the letter," said the barber.

Sancho put his hand into his pocket to get the notebook. He fumbled a great while without finding it. He searched first in one pocket, then in another. He searched in his sleeve, in his bosom, in his hat. But had he searched until now, he would not have found it. It had slipped through a hole in his pocket and was lost in the dust of the highway.

He turned pale, and his hands trembled. Then he began to rave, and to stamp like a madman. He tore his beard. He beat himself with his fists.

"Why need you be so angry, Sancho?" asked the curate, kindly. "What is the matter?"

"Matter enough," he answered. "I deserve the worst beating in the world, for I have lost three donkeys which were as good as three castles."

"How so?" asked the barber. "Were the donkeys in your pocket?"

"Not exactly," answered Sancho; "but I have lost the notebook which contained not only the letter to Dulcinea, but an order on Don Quixote's niece for three of his five donkeys."

Then with tears and sobs, the poor man told them how he had recently lost his own Dapple, the joy of his household, the hope of his life.

"Cheer up, Sancho," said the curate. "We are going to find your master, and I will see that he gives you another order written in due form on paper."

"Will you indeed?" said Sancho, brightening up. "Well then, the loss is not so bad after all. As for Dulcinea's letter, I don't care a straw about that. I know it all by heart, and will carry it to her by word of mouth. In other words, I will repeat it to her, just as it was written; and I will repeat it to you, if you wish."

"You speak like a wise man," said the curate. "But what concerns us now is to find your master and persuade him to give up his mad pranks and projects. So, come into the inn with us, and we'll talk it over while we eat dinner."

"You two may go in," answered Sancho; "but as for me, I feel best out here in the open air. However, you may send me a dish of hot victuals, if you like; and I will eat while I'm waiting. And you may tell the stable boy to bring Rozinante an armful of fodder."

So Sancho sat at the gate while the curate and the barber went inside. Presently a dish of hot meat was sent out to him, and he feasted as he had not feasted for many a day.

The hearty meal put him in fine, good humor; and as he thought over the words of the curate and the barber he made up his mind to return with them into the mountains. He was anxious to receive from Don Quixote a second order for the three donkeys.

He had scarcely finished his meal when the curate and the barber came riding out from the inn-yard, ready to begin the journey. No further time was wasted, and late that very afternoon they reached the place where Sancho had strewn the green branches in the road.

"It was right about here that I left him," he said.

And sure enough, they soon discovered the knight sitting quietly upon a rock and gazing at the sky. He was pale and almost starved, and Sancho could hear him sighing dolefully and muttering the name of the Lady Dulcinea.

I need not stop here to tell of the manner in which Don Quixote received his friends, who were so disguised that he did not know them; nor shall I describe the ingenious trick by which they induced him to put on his armor again and ride out of the forest.

At first, all went well; for he was persuaded that he was going to the aid of a fair princess whom a tyrant had driven from her kingdom.

"Come on," he cried, as he mounted Rozinante; "let us all go together and avenge the wrongs of this unfortunate lady."

They set out, the curate and the barber being disguised and unknown to their poor friend. Sancho was obliged to travel on foot again, while the rest rode gallantly along the highway on horseback. But his heart was light and free, and he kept thinking of the three donkeys and the glorious time when Don Quixote would make him the governor of an island.

The next day, when the party were well out of the mountains, they suddenly saw at a turn in the road, a stranger riding slowly along at a little distance ahead. He was dressed like a gypsy, and was mounted upon a small donkey which he could not by any means urge out of a snail's pace.

Sancho Panza's eyes opened very wide. For at the first glance he knew that the gypsy was none other than the thief, Gines de Passamonte, and that the donkey was his own long-lost Dapple.

The next moment he was running to overtake the pair; and although Gines tried hard to whip the donkey into a trot, Sancho was soon beside them.

"Ah, thou thief!" he shouted. "Get off from the back of my dear beast. Away from my Dapple! Away from my comfort! Take to thy heels and begone."

He had no need to use so many words. For Gines, seeing several men so close upon him, dismounted quickly and took to his heels. No doubt he thought that the king's officers were after him; for he bounded into the woods, and was soon out of sight.

And now Sancho's joy was too great to be described. He stroked the donkey with his hands; he kissed it again and again; he called it by every endearing name.

"My treasure, my darling, my dear Dapple! Is it possible that I have thee again? How hast thou been since I saw thee last?" he cried.

As for the donkey, it was as silent as any donkey could be. It said not one word in answer to Sancho's questions, but allowed him to kiss its nose as often as he pleased.

The rest of the company rejoiced at the squire's good fortune; and Don Quixote said: "I am glad that you have found your beast, Sancho. But it shall make no difference with the order which you have on my niece. She is to give you the three donkeys, just the same."

"I thank you, sir," said Sancho. "You were always a kind master."

16. The Ox-Cart Journey

THEY were still far from their home village, and Don Quixote's malady grew worse every day. He gave himself up to so many strange fancies that there was really no getting along with him. At length, when he would ride no farther in the right direction, the curate and the barber were forced to find some other plan by which to carry him home.

Luckily, one day, as they were stopping at an inn, a wagoner with his team of oxen came that way, looking for something to do. He was willing to undertake almost anything, and so the curate soon made a bargain with him.

With much labor and care, a sort of wooden cage was made which could be fastened firmly on the ox-driver's wagon. It was fitted up very comfortably with a stool and a cushion, and it was so high and roomy that a man might sit or lie in it with ease.

Don Quixote knew nothing about the plot which his friends were making against his liberty. While they were busy in the barnyard, he sat in the inn, and talked of knights and knighthood to everyone who would listen.

Late in the evening, as he lay quietly sleeping in his chamber, a number of strangely dressed men made their way softly to his door. They had masks on their faces; they wore long, white robes; and their whole appearance was very frightful indeed. They were the curate and the barber and the other guests of the inn; but they were so disguised that not even Sancho Panza could have guessed who they were.

They opened the chamber door and stole in. Don Quixote awoke with a start. He looked around him in amazement, but not in fear. When he saw the white-robed figures standing by his bedside, he sat up very quietly, and said not a word.

He felt sure that he was now in an enchanted castle, and that these figures were ghosts and hobgoblins which had been called up to frighten him. He knew that it was useless to fight with such creatures; for enchantment could be met only by enchantment. Therefore he quietly gave himself up, and made no resistance.

The hobgoblins lifted him out of bed. They dressed him in his best clothes. Then they carried him out and put him in the wooden cage which stood ready at the door. They shut him safely in, and fastened the bars securely.

The ox cart was waiting in the courtyard of the inn. The men lifted the cage upon it very gently and strapped it fast. Then the wagoner cracked his whip, and the oxen began to move slowly and solemnly towards the great gate.

Don Quixote was not altogether displeased. He spoke to the people, who had come out in the dim moonlight to see him depart.

"In all my books, I never read of a knight-errant being drawn in a slow-moving ox cart," he said. "They used to be whisked along with marvelous speed on winged steeds and other quick-going beasts. But this traveling in an ox cart is not so bad, and I don't object."

Having said this, he became very quiet, and did not speak again for a long time.

89

It was an odd-looking company that jogged along the road across the great plain the next day. The wagoner led the way with his oxen and his knightly prisoner. On either side of him rode an officer whose acquaintance the curate had made at the inn. Close behind the cart, followed Sancho, riding his dappled donkey and leading Rozinante. Lastly, the curate and the barber, with veiled faces and riding astride of mighty mules, brought up the rear.

Don Quixote sat, most of the time, leaning against the bars of the cage. He was free to move about or to lie down as he chose; but he sat silent and motionless, and seemed more like a lifeless statue than a living man. And thus they journeyed slowly over the long and seldom-traveled road.

As the day wore on, the heart of Sancho Panza was filled with pain because of his master's grievous plight. He could not bear to think of him thus caged like a wild beast and hauled from place to place against his will. So, while the guards were eating their noonday luncheon, he spent the hour in talking with Don Quixote.

The knight seemed more like himself, and he spoke very cheerfully with his squire.

"Good Sancho," he said, "have courage. I assure you that we shall soon escape from the power of these wicked enchanters."

"Well, master," said Sancho, "I'll tell you the plain truth about this enchantment. Who would you think now are those two fellows that ride behind with their faces covered?"

"Why, they are the enchanters, of course," answered Don Quixote.

"Enchanters never!" said Sancho. "They are only the curate of our village, and the barber. They are in a plot against you; for they fear that your brave deeds will make you more famous than they can ever be. There is no enchantment at all in this business. It's only your senses turned topsy-turvy."

"Friend Sancho," answered Don Quixote, "I tell you, it is enchantment; and the idea that those who guard us are my old friends, the curate and the barber, is a wicked delusion. The power of magic is great; and if these enchanters seem to be clothed in bodies like those of my friends, it proves only their skill and their wonderful ingenuity."

At length, by the curate's permission, Sancho opened the cage and helped his poor master to step out upon the ground.

"Come, sir," he said, "I will set you free from this prison. See now whether you can get on your trusty Rozinante's back. The poor thing jogs on, as drooping and sorrowful as if he too were enchanted."

"I will do as you say, friend Sancho," answered his master. "But I give my word of honor to these gentlemen that I will make no effort to escape. I desire only to ride my steed as becomes a true knight—that is, if I find myself strong enough to do so."

He walked feebly up to Rozinante and lovingly stroked his neck and back.

"Ah, thou flower and glory of horseflesh," he said, "I trust that we shall soon be ourselves again."

But his strength had all left him. Even when he was lifted into the saddle, he was too feeble to sit there. A dizziness came over him, and he remembered with longing his quiet home and his loving neighbors and friends.

"Help me once more into the enchanted car, friend Sancho," he said, "for I am not in a condition to press the back of Rozinante."

"With all my heart," said Sancho. "And let me advise you to go willingly back to our village with these gentlemen. At home we may plan some other journey that will be more profitable and perhaps more pleasant than this has been."

"Your advice is good," answered the knight. "But until this enchantment has been removed, I shall be inactive."

The wagoner threw some new-mown hay into the cage; then they lifted the knight gently and laid him upon this fragrant couch. They fastened no bars, but left the place open, so that he would not feel like a prisoner.

Then the wagoner cracked his whip, and the procession moved on as before. And thus they journeyed slowly along the seldom-traveled road across the hills and the plain.

It was about noon of the sixth day when they at length reached their home village. It was Sunday, and nearly all the people were on the street.

When the ox cart was seen, trundling along with a cage upon it, it was at once surrounded by a crowd of men and boys. All wanted to know what kind of show beast it was that was being thus hauled through the village.

What was their surprise, however, when they saw no beast at all, but only their honored neighbor and friend—the man whom they knew only by the name of Mr. Quixana!

He was lying on the hay and taking but little notice of anything around him. The village seemed strange to him, and the faces of his friends were unknown and unrecognized.

While the villagers were gaping and wondering, a little boy suddenly left the crowd and ran by the shortest way to Don Quixote's dwelling. He rushed into the house and cried out to the niece and housekeeper that their uncle and master was coming home and was almost at the door.

"And oh, he is so lean and pale!" piped the boy, all out of breath. "And he's on a bundle of hay in a big wagon, and the wagon is an ox cart. And you can soon see him for yourselves!"

The two women listened, and then it was piteous to hear their weeping.

"It's all on account of his reading those books," sobbed the niece.

"We ought to have made way with them long before," sighed the housekeeper.

The ox cart, with its honored passenger and faithful guards, moved slowly down the street, while the awed villagers followed silently and with much wonder. Suddenly a woman rushed from one of the cottages and ran out to meet the procession.

"Welcome, Sancho!" she cried. "How is the dear donkey?"

"The donkey has come back in better health than his master," answered the squire.

"How thankful I am for that!" said Juana. "But what have you brought home? Have you brought me a new petticoat, or the children some shoes?"

"In truth, sweet wife," said Sancho, "I have brought none of those things. But the next time we ride out, I shall return right soon, and you will find me the governor of an island. "

"I hope so, with all my heart," answered the good wife; "for surely we need it. But what do you mean by that word *island?* I never heard it before. I don't understand what sort of thing it is."

"All in good time, Juana," said Sancho. "Honey is not made for a donkey's mouth; but you shall see what sort of thing it is. And let me tell you, there is nothing so good for an honest man as to be the squire to a knight that is hunting adventures."

"Well, I'm glad you think so!" said she.

"Oh, I not only think, but I know it," said Sancho. "It's rare sport to climb mountains, to scramble over rocks, to beat through the woods, to visit great castles, and to put up at inns without a penny to pay."

By this time the ox cart, with its company of guards and villagers, had reached the door of Don Quixote's dwelling. The curate and the barber lifted the poor knight from his couch of hay, and carried him tenderly into his own chamber.

He was as helpless as a child, and neither spoke nor attempted to move. The housekeeper and the niece undressed him and put him in his ancient bed. He lay there, looking at them curiously and wondering who they were. Their faces seemed altogether strange to him. He could not imagine where he was.

The curate charged the niece to be very careful and tender of her uncle. "And by all means," he said, "be watchful lest he should try to ride out a third time in quest of adventures."

One by one, the good man's neighbors and friends returned to their homes. Sancho Panza, with his donkey, sought his own dwelling. And Don Quixote once more reposed quietly beneath his own roof.

17. With Friends and Neighbors

FOR nearly a month Don Quixote remained at home, seeing no one at all but his niece and the housekeeper. The curate and the barber came daily to inquire how he was doing; but they kept carefully out of his sight lest they might hinder his recovery.

At length the niece told them that he was well and in his right mind. Would they not come in and see him?

"With much pleasure," answered the barber; and they were ushered in.

They found the poor gentleman sitting up in his bed. He wore a waistcoat of green baize, and on his head was a red nightcap. His eyes were bright, and his voice was clear; but his face and body were so withered and wasted that he looked like a mummy.

He seemed glad to see his two old friends. They sat down by his bedside, and talked with him about a great many matters. They tried to say nothing about knight-errantry, but at last the subject came up in spite of them.

Then Don Quixote grew eloquent. He talked about knights and giants and famous heroes, scarcely giving the curate room to put in a word.

His friends saw with sadness that his mind still ran towards the same great passion. They saw that it was his intention, sooner or later, to ride out again to seek new adventures. So when at last they took their departure, the curate again whispered a word of caution to the niece.

"Keep a good watch upon him," he said. "Let everything be very quiet around him, and don't let him think about going away from home."

As Don Quixote improved in strength and became able to walk about the house, other neighbors and friends dropped in to see him. He welcomed each one cheerfully, and never failed to say something in praise of knighthood. But they, having been cautioned by the curate, talked to him only about the weather and the crops, and soon took their leave. And so the poor man gradually grew stronger and seemed to be quite well contented.

One morning, however, who should knock at the door but Sancho Panza.

"I have come to see the valorous Don Quixote," he said to the niece.

"You shall see nobody!" she answered, holding the door against him. "You shall not enter the house, you vagabond!"

"Go, go!" cried the housekeeper. "It's all along of you and nobody else, that he has been enticed and carried a-rambling all over the world."

"No such thing," answered Sancho. "It's I that have been enticed and carried a-rambling, and not your master. It was he that took me from house and home, saying he would give me an island; and I'm still waiting for it."

"An island! What's that?" said the niece. "If it's anything to eat, I hope it'll choke you."

"You're wrong there," answered Sancho. "Islands are not to eat; they're to govern."

"Well, anyhow, you don't come in here," said the niece. "Go govern your own house, plow your own field, and don't trouble yourself about anybody's islands and dry lands. They're not for such as you."

It so happened that the curate and the barber, who were just taking their leave after a short visit, heard the whole of this little quarrel. They were much amused by it, and were about to give their help to the niece when Don Quixote himself came to the door.

"Welcome, my faithful friend," he said; and giving his niece a sharp rebuke, he led Sancho into the house.

"Now mark me," whispered the curate, "our neighbor will soon be rambling again in spite of all that we can do."

Don Quixote led his squire into the bedroom and locked the door. Then the two sat down together and talked of the glories and perils of knighthood.

"What say you, friend Sancho?" said the knight. "Will you return to my service? What does your good wife say?"

"She says that a man must not be his own carver," answered Sancho. "She says that it is good to be certain; that a bird in the hand is worth two in the bush; that one hold-fast is better than two may-be-so's. A woman's counsel is not worth much, yet he that despises it is no better than he should be."

"I say so too," said Don Quixote. "You talk like pearls to-day. But what shall I understand from all that?"

"Why, sir," answered Sancho, "I wish you to give me so much a month for my wages. For other rewards come late, and may not come at all. A little in one's own pocket is better than much in another's purse. Set a hen upon an egg. Every little makes a mickle."

"You are wise, Sancho," said Don Quixote, "and I understand the drift of all your proverbs."

"Certainly," answered Sancho, "and I should like to know what I am going to get. If you should sometime give me that island, I would then be willing to knock a proper amount off of the wages."

"As to the wages," said Don Quixote, "I would pay them willingly if it were allowed by our order. But in all the books I have ever read, there is no account of a knight paying wages to his squire. The servant was always given an island, or something of that sort, and there was an end of it."

"But suppose that the island was not forthcoming?" said Sancho.

"I abide by the customs of chivalry," said Don Quixote, firmly. "If you desire not to take the same risks of fortune as myself, heaven be with you. I can find a squire more obedient and careful than you have ever been, and much less talkative."

Sancho's heart sank within him. He had not expected an answer like this. In fact he had thought that Don Quixote could not possibly do without him. He was so taken aback that he did not know what to say or do.

At that moment there was a knock at the door. It was opened, and in came the housekeeper and the niece, and with them a young man of the village whose name was Samson Carrasco.

This young man was just home from the great college at Salamanca, where he had received his bachelor's degree. He was none of the biggest in body, but a very great man in all sorts of drollery. He was about twenty-four years old; his face was round; his mouth was large; and his eyes sparkled with good humor.

"You are a scholar," whispered the niece, as they entered the room. "Try to persuade him from riding out again."

But Samson liked nothing so well as sport, and he was a great actor and mimic. He threw himself at Don Quixote's feet and delivered a speech that was full of flattery and big words.

"O flower of chivalry," he cried, "refulgent glory of arms, the pride of Spain! Let all who would prevent thy third going out be lost and disappointed in their perverse wishes."

Then, turning to the housekeeper, he said, "You must not detain him; for while he stays here idle, the poor are without a helper, orphans are without a friend, the oppressed are without a defender, and the world is deprived of a most valorous knight."

To this speech the housekeeper could make no reply, and Samson therefore turned again to Don Quixote.

"Go forth then, my graceful, my fearless hero," he said. "Let your greatness be on the wing. And if anything be needful to your comfort or your service, here I am to supply it. I am ready to do anything. I am ready, yes, ambitious, to attend you as your squire and faithful servant."

Don Quixote was deeply moved. He took the young man by the hand, and embraced him. "No, my friend," he said, "it would be unfair that Samson Carrasco, the darling of courts and the glory of the Salamanca schools, should devote his talents to such a purpose. I forbid it. Remain in thy country, the honor of Spain and the delight of thy parents. Although Sancho declines to go with me, there are plenty of others who will be glad to serve as my squire.

At these words Sancho burst into tears and cried out, "Oh, I'll go! I'll go with you, sir! I have not a heart of flint; and if I spoke about wages, it was only to please my wife."

So the two embraced, and were as good friends as before; and with the advice of Samson Carrasco it was agreed that on the third day they would set out on their new trial of adventures.

The niece and the housekeeper made a woeful out-cry. They tore their hair. They scratched their faces. They scolded; they pleaded; they wept bitter tears. But nothing could change the designs of the valorous knight.

The curate and the barber, as well as the women, blamed Samson Carrasco for the whole business. But he understood the case better than they. "It is wiser not to restrain him," he said. "He will find the cure for his malady not here, but on the road. So let us humor him."

99

18. In Search of Dulcinea

TOWARDS evening on the appointed day, the start was made. Don Quixote mounted his Rozinante, and Sancho threw himself astride of his faithful Dapple. The knight carried a new lance and wore a new helmet of brass which his friend Samson had given him; and the squire carried a wallet well filled with provisions, and a purse stuffed with money to defray expenses.

The niece and the housekeeper, having become reconciled to the journey, stood at the door, waving their good-bys; and Sancho's wife, watching from her window, wept her farewells as they passed. Samson Carrasco walked with them to the edge of the village, and there bade them Godspeed on their journey.

And so, knight and squire rode forth with solemn faces and high resolves, ready to encounter whatever fate was in store for them.

"Friend Sancho," said Don Quixote, "our first duty is plain. Before undertaking any feat of arms we must repair to the city of Toboso and there perform those acts of homage which are due to the peerless Lady Dulcinea."

"It is even as you command, Sir Knight," answered Sancho.

Therefore, to Toboso they made their way.

It was late in the afternoon of the second day when they came in sight of that notable and most important place. Since Don Quixote did not know the house in which Dulcinea lived, he thought it best to tarry outside until after nightfall. They therefore spent the evening under some oaks a little way from the road, and did not enter Toboso until about midnight.

As they rode along the grass-grown street, the whole world seemed silent. There was no one stirring in the city. The people were all asleep; there was no light save that of the moon. The heart of Don Quixote was filled with forebodings.

"My dear Sancho," he whispered hoarsely, "show me the way to her palace."

"Palace!" said Sancho. "What palace do you mean? When I saw her, she was living in a small cottage."

Now, in truth, he had never seen her at all; but he wished to make believe that he had done so when his master had sent him with the letter.

They rode slowly along the street until they approached a large building, which loomed tall and dark in the dim moonlight.

"Here it is," said Don Quixote. "Here is my Dulcinea's palace, and it is well worthy of the peerless lady."

But when he rode up closer, he discovered that it was no palace at all, but only the great church of the town.

"We have made a mistake, Sancho," he said. "This is not her dwelling place, and we shall have to look farther."

They rode onward to the end of the street. Then they came back and looked through every by-path and alley, but they could not find anything that looked like a palace.

Presently the night began to wear away. A faint light appeared in the east; it grew larger and brighter; it overspread the sky. The swallows that were nesting under the eaves began to twitter. Morning was nigh at hand.

Here and there a door was heard to open. The sound of voices broke the stillness of the town. The people were beginning to stir.

As knight and squire paused in the street, uncertain what to do, a young countryman came along, driving a pair of mules and singing the song of Roland. "Good morning, honest friend," said Don Quixote. "Pray tell me, where is the palace of the peerless princess, the Lady Dulcinea del Toboso?"

"Sir," answered the young fellow, "I've just lately come to Toboso, and I don't know of any palaces. But the curate of the town lives in this next house. Ask him. He knows all about princesses and palaces."

Having said this, he switched his mules and drove on, singing louder than before. Don Quixote, sitting quietly on the back of Rozinante, gazed at the curate's house, uncertain what to do. Curates were not always favorable to chivalry, and this curate might not sympathize with a wandering knight, however valorous he might be.

It was now broad daylight. The sun was almost above the trees. There would soon be other passers-by in the street. Sancho Panza began to feel uneasy.

"I think, sir," said he, "that it will not be very handsome for us to sit here and be stared at by everybody in the town. We had better slip out to some grove not far away. Then while you lie there hidden, I will come back and search every hole and corner for the Lady Dulcinea. When I find her, I'll talk to her and tell her that you are close by, waiting for her orders. This, of course, will make her all the more ready to receive you."

"Dear Sancho," answered Don Quixote, "you, were always wise. You have said a thousand sentences in a few words, and I will do exactly as you say."

Without further loss of time, therefore, they turned their steeds about and rode out of town to a grove some two miles away. There Don Quixote concealed himself among the trees bidding Sancho Panza return and make haste to discover the whereabouts of the Lady Dulcinea.

"Cheer up, master!" Sancho replied at leaving. "I'll be back here in a trice. The hare leaps out of the bush where we least expect her. Faint heart never won fair lady."

"Sancho," said the knight, "you have a rare talent for quoting proverbs." But the squire was already riding briskly away towards the town.

He did not ride far, however. At the foot of a little hill he paused and looked back. Seeing that he was out of his master's sight, he stopped under a tree by the roadside, and began to talk with himself.

"Friend Sancho, where are you going? Are you hunting for a mule?"

"No; not for any mule."

"What, then, are you doing?"

"I am looking for a princess who is the sum of all beauty."

"Where do you think you will find her?"

"Where? Why, in the great city of Toboso. But it's like looking for a needle in a haystack."

"Why do you undertake such a thing?"

"Why? To please my mad master, of course. But if he is mad enough to mistake windmills for giants, it will not be hard to make him believe that any country girl is the Lady Dulcinea."

"Certainly, it will not."

"Well, that is just what I'll do. It will be the easiest way out of this troublesome business."

So he alighted and sat down under the tree. The shade was pleasant, and he remembered the provisions which he had in his wallet. When he had eaten a hearty breakfast, he lay down and slept until it was far past midday.

At last he awoke feeling rested and contented. "This is better than riding through Toboso, hunting for Dulcinea's palace," he said.

He had just remounted his donkey when, looking down the road, he saw three country girls coming up from the town. They were awkward and red-faced, and were riding slowly along on donkeys.

Sancho did not wait a moment, but turned his steed quickly about and made all haste back to his master.

"Well, my good Sancho, what news?" asked the knight, eagerly. "Are we to mark this day with a white stone or with a black?"

"Mark it with red ocher, sir," answered Sancho. "The Lady Dulcinea with her two maids is coming out to meet you. She is close at hand even now. So, mount

Rozinante quickly, and get into the road where you can see her for yourself and greet her in a becoming manner."

"I can hardly believe such news, Sancho," said Don Quixote. "Do not add to my grief by deceiving me."

"Deceive you, sir? Why should I wish to play a trick on you? Come, ride out with me quickly, and you will see the princess coming. She and her damsels are all one sparkle of gold—all pearls, all diamonds, all rubies. There was never so much beauty seen in Spain."

"Let us hasten then, Sancho," said Don Quixote, climbing upon Rozinante with uncommon speed. "And I promise to reward you for your good news. You shall have the best spoils of our next adventure; and if that is not enough, I will give you the three colts I have at home."

"I shall be very glad to get the colts, master, and I thank you," said Sancho; "but as for spoils, they are so small that I'm not particular."

They rode hastily out of the grove and were soon on the highroad at the crest of the hill. Looking down towards the town, they could see no one but the three country lasses approaching slowly on their donkeys.

Don Quixote's face showed his deep disappointment. He paused and looked backward and forward, this way and that.

"I don't see her, Sancho," he said. "Are you sure that she has left the city?"

"Why, where are your eyes, master?" answered the squire. "Don't you see her right here with her two lovely maidens?"

"I see nothing but three country girls on three very scrawny donkeys."

"Well! well! Is it possible that you mistake the princess for an awkward country girl? Can't you distinguish a beautiful palfrey from a miserable donkey?"

"To tell you the truth, Sancho, I see nothing but three donkeys carrying as many red-faced country girls. They are coming towards us, and I see them quite plainly. But where is the princess?"

"Oh, master, master! How blind you are! There is no country girl in sight. It is the princess whom you see, and she is drawing nearer every moment. Let us hasten and speak to her."

So saying, Sancho spurred his donkey onward, and hurried down the hill to meet the girls. He leaped to the ground in the middle of the road before them. He placed himself in front of the tallest and most ungainly of the three. He lifted his hat and fell upon his knees.

"Queen and princess of beauty, listen to my prayer," he began. "If it please your highness and haughtiness, grant to take into your liking yonder knight who is your humble captive. I am Sancho Panza, his famous squire, and he is the wandering, weather-beaten Don Quixote de la Mancha."

By this time Don Quixote had also dismounted and was kneeling in the middle of the road. It was hard for him to believe that this homely damsel was his queen, the Lady Dulcinea; for she was flat-nosed and blubber-cheeked and coarse in form and manners. Yet he tried to imagine that some enchanter had changed her into this form.

"Get out of our way!" screamed the angry girls. "We're in a hurry to get home."

But Sancho knelt unmoved in the very pathway of their mules. "Oh, universal lady," he said, "does not your heart melt in pity? See there, how the post and pillar of knight-errantry is offering his homage to you."

"Heyday!" cried one of the girls. "Listen to his gibberish!"

"Get out of the way," shouted the tall one.

"Yes, get out of the way, and let us get along!" screamed the third.

With that, they kicked their donkeys in the ribs and crowded past. The next moment they were speeding away in a cloud of dust and were soon at the top of the hill.

Don Quixote rose from the ground and looked after them. He watched them with sorrowing eyes until a turn in the road hid them from sight. Then he turned to the squire, and said:—

"Sancho, what do you think of this business? Aren't those enchanters the most evil-minded creatures you ever saw? They were not content with turning my Dulcinea into the likeness of a coarse country girl; they went so far as to take from her the sweet perfume of flowers. For didn't you notice that strong whiff of raw onions as she passed us? It almost took my breath away."

"Oh, those enchanters!" cried Sancho. "They don't stop at any kind of wickedness. I wish I could see them all strung on a thread and hung up to dry, like a lot of herrings."

"Ah, well, well!" sighed Don Quixote. "I have said it before, and now I say it a thousand times: I am the most unlucky man in the universe."

Then he remounted Rozinante, and rode on, very sad and silent. He rode on through the town and down the long, dusty highway on the other side, not caring whither he went. And Sancho Panza followed him.

19. The Strolling Players

A FEW DAYS afterward as Don Quixote was riding onward and still grieving because of his ill luck, he suddenly met a large cart full of strange people.

The driver, who was walking by his horses, was dressed very oddly. His coat and trousers were of scarlet, he had horns on his head, and he wore a long pointed tail.

"He looks like some wicked hobgoblin," whispered Sancho to his master.

Seated in the cart there was a hideous figure of Death. On one side of this figure, an angel was standing with its great white wings folded. On the other side sat an emperor with a golden crown on his head.

Behind these there was a Cupid with bow and arrows, as Cupids always are. And near him was a knight in white armor who wore a soft hat instead of a helmet.

Following the cart on foot, there came a clown with cap and bells; and with him were three or four other persons dressed in strange and brightly colored clothing.

Neither knight nor squire had ever seen so strange a company of travelers, and Don Quixote paused in surprise at meeting them in that lonely place. As for Sancho, he was frightened beyond measure; for he thought that these were the enchanters, of whom his master was always talking, and no mistake.

Soon, however, Don Quixote's face grew brighter, for a brave thought had come to him. He spurred Rozinante forward, saying to Sancho, "Perhaps this will be the rarest of all our adventures."

He planted himself in the middle of the road before the approaching company. Then he shouted, "You carter, coachman, or whatever you be, halt! Halt there, and answer my questions. Who are you? Where have you come from? Whither are you going? What is your business?"

The driver brought the cart to a standstill, and looked up with surprise at the strangely clad horseman who had thus challenged him.

"Sir," he said, "we are a party of players. We have just come from the town on the other side of the mountain, where we have been playing a tragedy called the Dance of Death. This afternoon we are to play it again in the next town. We are traveling in our acting clothes, so as to save the trouble of dressing and undressing ourselves."

"You speak like an honest man," said Don Quixote, "although you look like something quite different."

"Well, I play the part of the devil," answered the driver, "and you know that is the best part of all. The young man in the wagon takes the part of Death, and the person by his side is an angel. Then there is the emperor, and there is the soldier, and behind the wagon you can see all the rest of the company."

"I wish you well, good people," said Don Quixote, moving aside. "Drive on now, and act your play. If I can be of any help to you, I shall be much pleased; for even in my childhood, I loved the player's art."

At this moment the clown came frisking to the front of the wagon to see what was going on. A number of tinkling bells were fastened to his coat; and he had a long stick with three bladders on it, which he flourished back and forth in the air.

His first act was to bounce the bladders right under poor Rozinante's nose. This so startled the old horse that he sprang forward, and quickly had the better of his rider. He took the bit in his teeth, and ran, with all the speed of a plow horse, across the open field.

Sancho was in great fear lest Don Quixote should be thrown and hurt. He therefore leaped from his donkey and gave chase, hoping to overtake the fleeing steed, or at the worst, to ease his master's fall. But before he had gone a hundred yards, Rozinante stumbled, and horse and rider fell rolling in the dust.

Now the clown, when he saw Sancho dismount, ran hastily to the dappled donkey and leaped upon its back. He rattled the bladders over the poor creature's ears, and so frightened it that it went flying down the road towards the town where the play was to be.

Sancho, seeing this, was uncertain what to do. Should he help his master, or should he run after Dapple and the clown? He turned this way, he turned that; he leaped over the fence, he leaped back; and at last he hurried to the knight and helped him to rise.

"Oh, sir!" he cried, "the evil one has run away with my dear Dapple."

"What evil one?" asked Don Quixote.

"Why, the one with the bladders," answered Sancho.

"Well, don't grieve about that," said Don Quixote, " I'll force him to give the animal up. Follow me, Sancho."

"Oh, master, I'd rather not," said Sancho. "Anyhow, we needn't be in a hurry; for I see that he has now left the donkey and gone his way."

What he said was true, for the donkey had fallen in the road and thrown its rider. The clown picked himself up, unhurt, and walked on towards the town. The donkey also arose, and after looking around, came slowly back toward its master.

"All this is lucky for you," said Don Quixote, "but it won't hinder me from teaching those people a lesson."

Then, in spite of all that Sancho could do or say, he galloped after the cart, crying, "Hold, hold! Stop there, my pretty sparks. I'll teach you to be a little more civil to strangers when you meet them on the road."

The players stopped. They leaped out of the wagon, and ranged themselves by the side of the road. Each had a stone in his hand ready, in case of need, to let fly at the knight and his squire.

Don Quixote checked his flying steed. He paused for a moment to think of the best way to attack this fearless company. He raised his lance and was just going to charge upon his foes, when Sancho overtook him.

"For goodness' sake, sir," he cried, "are you mad? Leave those fellows alone. They are only players, and there's not a single knight among them."

"There, there!" answered Don Quixote. "You have touched me upon the only point that can move me. For indeed it would never do for me to engage in combat with any but true knights. You are the man, Sancho, to fight with players. It is your business. So, get at them! I will stay here and help you with good advice."

109

"No, I thank you, sir," said Sancho. "I forgive those people. I like nothing so well as peace and quiet. And, in fact, the donkey has not been hurt at all. So why should we make a fuss about it?"

"Oh, well," answered his master, "if that's the way you feel about it, friend Sancho, we had better leave them alone. Come! Mount your donkey, and let us ride onward in search of more worthy adventures."

So saying he wheeled his steed about, and resumed his journey. And Sancho, well pleased and very meek, mounted Dapple and followed him.

20. The Knight of the Mirrors

THAT night Don Quixote and Sancho Panza sought shelter under some trees by the roadside. Sancho unsaddled his Dapple and turned the beast loose to graze among the shrubs and thistles; then he threw himself down at the foot of a cork tree and was soon fast asleep.

But poor Rozinante was doomed to stand saddled all night; for his master suddenly remembered that it was the custom of knights-errant to take off only the bridles of their steeds when thus resting in the open air.

Don Quixote lay down beneath a spreading oak tree and tried to compose himself to rest. He lay and watched the stars twinkling in the sky above him, and he tried to remember all the noble knights who had likewise reposed at night under the canopy of a tree. Suddenly he was aroused by hearing a noise near him. He sat up and listened.

He heard voices in the road. He heard them approaching the grove of trees.

Soon he was aware that two men on horseback were close at hand. He could see only their shadowy figures in the midsummer darkness as they came slowly toward his resting place. Then he could distinguish what they said.

"Let us alight here, friend," said one. "Me-thinks this is a pleasant place to rest for the night."

Don Quixote, watching from the shadows of the oak, saw him slide carelessly from his horse and throw himself down in the tall grass. He heard a rattling like that of armor; he thought he saw the dim outlines of a shield; and all this filled his heart with joy.

"This stranger is a knight like myself," he thought.

Then, with the greatest caution, he went softly over to the cork tree and woke his squire.

"Sancho," he whispered, "wake up! Here is an adventure for us."

"Well, I hope it is a good one," said Sancho. "Where is it?"

"Where? Only turn your head, man, and look yonder. There is a knight-errant lying in the grass. I think he is melancholy, for I heard him sigh as he slid from his horse."

"Well, what of that? How do you make an adventure out of it, even if he did sigh?"

"I'm not sure it is an adventure," answered Don Quixote; "but it looks that way. Hark! He is sitting up now, and tuning his guitar. He is going to sing."

They sat and listened. Soon the voice of the strange knight was heard mingling with the sweet thrumming tones of the guitar.

"What! what!" whispered Don Quixote. "He is singing of the cruelty of his lady love. Didn't I tell you he was melancholy?"

When the knight had finished his song he began to sigh most dolefully. He arose, and leaning against a tree, cried out in a mournful voice, "Oh, thou fair Casildea de Vandalia, thou fairest of the fair! Is it not enough to be known as the fairest lady in the world? For all the brave knights of Castile and Leon and La Mancha declare that thou hast no equal in beauty and queenly grace."

"It is not so," said Don Quixote, speaking softly to Sancho. "I am the only knight of La Mancha, and I have never said, nor shall I ever

say that any lady is as beautiful as my own Dulcinea. It is plain that this knight is out of his senses. But let us listen. We shall hear more."

"Yes, I think we shall hear enough," answered Sancho; "for he seems likely to keep on grumbling for a month."

He spoke so loudly that the strange knight heard him. "Who's there?" he called, coming out from the shadows.

"Friends," answered Sancho.

"Are you of the happy, or of the miserable?" asked the knight.

"The miserable! the miserable!" answered Don Quixote.

"Then I welcome you," said the stranger. "Come over here and sit with me."

Don Quixote went over. The knight shook hands with him and seemed very glad.

"I am a knight," said Don Quixote.

"And so am I," answered the other.

Then they sat down in the grass and talked together very peaceably and lovingly, and not at all like two men who were going to break each other's heads.

In the meanwhile Sancho went across the road to the spot where the strange knight's squire was resting by the side of his steed.

"Hello, stranger!" he said.

"Hello to you, my friend," said the other. "Sit down here, and let us chat freely to ourselves, just as squires always do."

"With all my heart," answered Sancho. "I'll talk with you, and tell you who I am and what I am. Then you will know whether I'm fit to be a squire or not."

So the two sat down by the trunk of a tree and for some time talked as foolishly as their masters were talking wisely.

The hours wore pleasantly on under the starry sky. The two squires soon dropped asleep, and lay snoring side by side on the warm earth. But the two knights were so full of talk that they never thought of slumber; and many were the tales of valor which each related to the other.

The strange knight was a great boaster. There was no war in which he had not fought; there was no trial of arms in which he had not been the victor. "I reckon that I have vanquished every wandering knight in the universe," he said. "I once jousted with the renowned Don Quixote de la Mancha and overcame him in fair combat."

"Hold!" cried Don Quixote in wonder and anger. "Don't say that! You may have vanquished all the knights in Spain, save one; but you have never encountered Don Quixote."

"But I say that I have," answered the stranger.

"Perhaps you have fought with some one who looks like him," said Don Quixote; "but had you met the man himself, you would not now be boasting of your encounter."

"What do you mean?" cried the stranger, rising to his feet. "I tell you that it was Don Quixote himself whom I vanquished. There is no one who looks like him. He is a tall, slim-faced, leather-jawed fellow. His hair is grizzled. He is hawk-nosed. He has a long, lank mustache. The name of his squire is Sancho Panza; and the name of his lady is Dulcinea del Toboso. Now, if you don't believe me, let me say that I wear a sword and I will make you believe."

"Not so fast, Sir Knight," answered Don Quixote. "I am acquainted with this same valorous knight of La Mancha. In fact he is the best friend I have in the world, and I love him as well as I love myself. You have described him well; but you have never fought with him. The enchanters, who are his enemies, have probably made some other knight look like him."

The stranger shook his head.

"It is even so," continued Don Quixote. "Indeed, it was not many days ago that they transformed the beautiful Dulcinea del Toboso into the ugly image of a coarse country girl. But if you still insist that you really overcame Don Quixote, let me tell you something: Here is that renowned knight himself, ready to make good his words either on foot or on horseback or in any other way you choose!"

As he said this, he jumped up and laid his hand on his sword. But the strange knight sat still on the ground.

"Sir," he said quietly, "if I could vanquish Don Quixote when transformed why shall I fear him in his true shape? But knights do not fight in the dark. Let us wait till morning, so that the sun may behold our valor."

"You speak well," answered Don Quixote; "I am willing to wait."

Having come to an agreement, the two knights, went across the road to look for their squires. They found them stretched on the ground and snoring. They roused them and bade them get their steeds ready; for with the rising of the sun the combat was to begin.

Sancho Panza was astounded at this news; but he said not a word. He went at once with the strange squire to look for the horses.

"Well, friend," said the other, "since our masters are going to fight, I guess that you and I must also have a brush. That is the way they do in Andalusia where I came from. Servants never stand idle while their masters are fighting."

"They may follow that custom in Andalusia," answered Sancho, "but I'm sure I won't follow it. I'm no hand at fighting. I never had a sword in my life."

"Oh, never mind the swords," said the strange squire. "I have a couple of bags here. You take one, and I'll take one, and we'll let drive at each other."

"That's good," cried Sancho. "We'll dust each other's jackets and not get hurt."

"Hardly so good as that," said the stranger. "We'll put half a dozen stones in each bag, so that we may fight the better."

"Then I say again that I don't feel like fighting," said Sancho. "Let us live and be merry while we may. I'm not angry with you, and I can't fight in cold blood."

"Oh, if that's all," said the other, "I can soon warm your blood. For, you see, I'll walk up to you quite gently and give you three or four slaps on the head and knock you down. Your blood will begin to boil then, won't it?"

"Boil or no boil, I'll meet you at that trick," answered Sancho. "I'll break your head with a stick. Every man for himself. Many come for wool and go home shorn. A baited cat may prove as fierce as a lion. Nobody knows what I may do when I'm stirred up."

By this time they had found the horses and were grooming them for the combat.

"Well, well! May the sun hasten to rise," said the strange squire. "I can hardly wait to begin the fight."

And in fact it was not long until the day began to break. Through the gray light of the dawn Sancho looked at his companion. His heart leaped with surprise, and he began to tremble. For he saw that the nose of the stranger was the most wonderful and fearful that could be imagined.

It was so big that it overshadowed the rest of his face. It was crooked in the middle and as red as a tomato.

"I would rather be kicked two hundred times than fight with that nose," said Sancho.

It was quite different with Don Quixote. He stood up boldly and gazed at the knight with whom he was about to fight. But the stranger's helmet was closed and he could not see his face.

His armor, however, was of the best fashion, and over it he wore a coat of cloth of gold. This was covered with numbers of tiny mirrors shaped like half moons.

The plume in his helmet was of yellow, green, and white feathers. His lance was very thick and long. The knight himself was slender, but shapely and quick of motion.

"Sir Knight of the Mirrors," said Don Quixote, "be pleased to lift up your helmet a little, so that I may see your face."

"Nay," answered the knight, "I cannot satisfy your curiosity now. After the combat you will have plenty of time to look at my face. But see, it is broad daylight. Let us begin."

115

"I am ready," answered Don Quixote. "But while we are getting on horseback, please tell me if I look like that Don Quixote whom you say you overthrew in fair fight."

"Certainly," said the Knight of the Mirrors, "You are as like him as one egg is like another."

"Then let us begin the business," said Don Quixote. "I'll soon show you that I'm not the Quixote whom you think."

116

So, without further words, they mounted. They rode some distance apart, and then wheeled about with their horses and made ready to charge.

At that moment, however, Don Quixote chanced to see the big nose of the strange squire. He paused in wonder, while the Knight of the Mirrors waited impatiently for him to begin the onset. Sancho Panza, seeing his master's surprise, ran up and caught hold of his stirrup.

"Please, dear master," he said, "before you run upon your enemy, help me up into this cork tree. I wish to sit where I can see your brave battle."

"I rather think you wish to be perched out of danger," said Don Quixote.

"To tell you the truth, master, I am a little afraid of that nose," said Sancho.

"I blame you not," answered Don Quixote. "It is indeed a sight to strike terror into any heart less brave than my own. So, put your foot in this stirrup, and then swing lightly up among the branches."

In the meanwhile the Knight of the Mirrors had again wheeled his horse about, and losing all patience, he now charged at full speed down upon his unready foe.

His steed, however, was old and shabby, in fact more so than Rozinante, and even with much spurring and urging, his swiftest speed was only a slow trot. Down the road he came, lumbering awkwardly and stumbling at every step; but at the middle of the course, his rider pulled suddenly upon the reins and he stopped short.

At this moment Don Quixote looked up. Seeing his enemy so near, he put spurs to Rozinante so sharply that the poor beast sprang wildly forward and, for the first time in his life, really galloped.

Before the Knight of the Mirrors could get his horse to moving again, Don Quixote dashed furiously upon him. The knight's lance was hurled from his grasp, and he himself was knocked out of his saddle and thrown sprawling in the dust. He was so stunned by the fall that he lay for some time without showing any signs of life.

Sancho had watched the short affray from his perch in the tree. He now slid down as quickly as he could, and ran to the help of his master.

As for Don Quixote, he checked his steed, threw himself from his saddle, and hurried to the side of his fallen foe. He unlaced the knight's helmet, to give him air, and gently lifted it from his head.

Who can relate his surprise when he saw the face of the unlucky Knight of the Mirrors? For there he beheld the very visage, the very aspect, the very features of his friend and neighbor, Samson Carrasco of La Mancha!

"See here, Sancho!" he cried. "See what those enchanters have been doing again."

Sancho looked and turned pale with fear.

"Master, take my advice," he whispered. "This is one of those enchanters who are all the time making trouble for you. He has now taken the form of our friend Samson Carrasco in order to injure both him and you. Run your sword down his throat, and so rid the world of at least one of the vile crew."

"That's a good thought, Sancho," answered Don Quixote. "I'll do as you say, and then we'll have fewer enemies."

With that, he drew his sword and was about to strike, when a voice at his elbow cried out, "Hold, Don Quixote!"

He looked around. There stood the strange squire, but his terrible nose had vanished.

"Have a care, Don Quixote," he said. "This fallen knight is your friend, Samson Carrasco, and I am his squire."

"Where is your nose?" asked Sancho.

"In my pocket," answered the squire; and he pulled out a great nose of varnished pasteboard.

"Why! why! why! Bless me!" cried Sancho. "Who is this? My old friend and neighbor, Thomas Cecial! Is it you, Tom?"

"The very same, friend Sancho," was the answer. "We have followed you all the way from La Mancha; and this is a trick we had planned to frighten Don Quixote and so persuade him to go back home."

"And you're not an enchanter?"

"I am only Thomas Cecial, your friend and neighbor. Look at me."

By this time the Knight of the Mirrors had come to himself. He groaned and looked around; then he sat up on the ground.

Don Quixote set the point of his sword against his face, and cried out, "Now confess that Dulcinea del Toboso is the most beautiful lady in the world. Confess it, or die."

"I do confess it," answered the knight. "The lady Dulcinea's old shoe is more beautiful than my Casildea."

"Will you go to the city of Toboso and confess it to my Dulcinea herself?"

"I will do anything that you command."

"Do you also confess that you never vanquished Don Quixote in fight, but only somebody else who looked like him?"

"All this I do confess, believe, and feel," said the fallen knight.

Then Don Quixote helped him to rise. He grasped his hand and shook it heartily.

"You look like my friend Samson Carrasco," he said, "but I know you are not he. You are some other man whom the enchanters have made to wear his countenance in order to deceive me. But I understand their tricks. They don't fool me."

Samson Carrasco was much put out. His carefully planned scheme to persuade his old neighbor to return home had failed at the very start. Don Quixote would not listen to him, nor believe that he was aught but some stranger in the service of the enchanters, or some poor knight who had been duped by them.

So, at length, with battered body and a sore heart, Samson remounted his sorry steed. Then, with his squire beside him, he rode painfully away toward the nearest town, where he hoped to find plasters and ointments for his bruises.

"I half believe it is really our friend Samson," said Sancho.

"Be not deceived by appearances, Sancho," answered his master.

Then they mounted their steeds and renewed their journey.

21. The Adventure with the Lions

THE sun rose high in the sky, and Don Quixote jogged onward, full of joy and pride. He had overthrown the Knight of the Mirrors, and he was more persuaded than ever that he was the most valiant hero in the world. Neither enchanter nor enchantments could alarm him. He was not afraid of anything whether real or unreal.

"Now, come what will come," he cried, "here I am, and I challenge the most powerful foes to meet me in combat."

About the middle of the afternoon, he was surprised to see in the distance a large wagon coming down the road from the opposite direction. As it drew nearer he saw that it was drawn by two mules and that several little flags were fluttering above it.

"See, Sancho! Here is an adventure for us," he said joyfully.

But Sancho shook his head doubtfully.

"Those are the king's flags," he said, "and they are to show that the wagon is carrying something for the king. It is best to be careful."

The strange vehicle was now close at hand. Only two men were with it: the wagoner who was astride of one of the mules, and a middle-aged man who sat on the top of the wagon.

Don Quixote rode briskly forward to meet them.

"What wagon is this?" he cried. "Who are you? Where are you going? What do those flags mean?"

"The wagon is mine," answered the man on the mule. "We have two lions in it, which the governor of Oran is sending to the king."

"Are the lions large?" asked Don Quixote.

"Very large," answered the man on the wagon. "They are the biggest ever seen in Spain, and I am their keeper. The he-lion is in the foremost cage, and the she-lion is in another cage at the rear of the wagon."

"That is right," said Don Quixote. "I see that you know how to manage wild beasts."

"The lions are hungry now, for they have not been fed to-day," said the keeper. "So, my good friend, please ride out of the way; for we are going to stop under this tree and give them their dinner. They are apt to be cross while eating."

"What!" cried Don Quixote, going up closer. "Shall I ride out of the way for lions? And at this time of day? I'll show you that I'm not afraid of such puny beasts. Get down, honest fellow, and open their cages. I'll soon show the creatures who I am. For I am the most valorous of all knights. Don Quixote de la Mancha."

Sancho had now come up; and when he heard this boastful speech he was frightened almost out of his wits.

"Oh, my good sir!" he cried to the keeper, "for pity's sake, don't let my master fall upon those lions. We shall all be eaten up."

"Why," said the keeper, "is your master so mad that he will dare to meddle with these beasts?"

"Ah, sir!" answered Sancho, "he is not mad, but rash, very rash!"

By this time the wagon had stopped, and Don Quixote was growing impatient.

"You rascal!" he cried, turning again to the keeper. "Do you hear me? Open your cages at once, or I'll pin you to the wagon with my lance."

The wagoner, who had leaped to the ground, was by nature a coward; and he was now almost helpless with fright.

"For mercy's sake," he cried, "let me take my mules out first. Let me get them out of the way before you open the cage. They are all that I have in the world."

"Thou man of little faith," said Don Quixote, "unhitch the poor things and take them away as quickly as possible. You will soon see that I am fully able to take care of the lions."

The wagoner hastened to obey. He loosed his mules from the wagon and then drove them with such speed as he could to the top of a hillock a quarter of a mile away. There, feeling himself safe, he paused to see what would happen.

In the meanwhile, Don Quixote again addressed the keeper.

"Obey me instantly," he said, "or suffer the punishment you deserve."

The keeper felt the point of the lance against his breast. He was by no means a brave man, and he turned pale as he realized the danger he was in.

"I will do as you bid me," he said, "but know all men that I am forced to turn the lions loose against my will."

Then he went around to the foremost cage and began to unfasten the door. "Shift for yourselves, all of you," he cried. "The lions know me and won't hurt me; but I won't answer for the harm they may do to others."

Then he again tried to reason with Don Quixote. "Sir, you are tempting Heaven by putting yourself in such danger," he said.

"You rascal," answered the knight, "it is for you to obey and not to advise. Open the cage, I say."

Then Sancho spoke up. "Good master," he said, "this is no trick of enchantment; it's the real thing. I've just taken a peep at the cage, and I saw the lion's claw. It's a tremendous big thing. The beast that owns it must be fully as big as a mountain."

"Your fears will make it as big as the world," answered Don Quixote. "Now, friend Sancho, retire to a place of safety and leave this business to me. If I fall in the conflict, you know your duty: carry the news to Dulcinea—I say no more."

Poor Sancho's eyes were full of tears, for he felt sure that his master was lost. He put spurs to his donkey and so joined the wagoner on the hillock of safety.

The keeper was now standing with his hand upon the cage door; and Don Quixote paused, uncertain whether he ought to fight on horseback or on foot.

"Rozinante is not used to lions, and he might not behave well," he said to himself. "I think it will be better to fight on foot."

He therefore dismounted and tied his horse to a tree. Then he laid aside his lance, and drew his sword.

The keeper advanced and with great caution opened the cage door, while Don Quixote with wondrous courage went forward and stood before it.

"Come out, thou paltry beast!" he cried. "Come out, and I will show thee what the bravest knight in the universe can do."

The lion turned himself around in the cage. He stretched out one of his paws. He gaped, and thrust out his tongue, which seemed as long as a man's arm.

The knight stood up very straight and again addressed the beast. "I challenge thee to come out and engage in fair combat with one who has never yet been vanquished, even with the renowned Don Quixote de la Mancha."

The lion, with his two great eyes that were like live coals, gazed steadily at him through the dim light in the cage. It was a sight to strike terror into the heart of any man; but Don Quixote felt no fear.

"I am ready for thee," he cried.

The generous lion took no notice of his words, but yawned again, and then lay down as if to take a nap.

"Do you see that?" said the keeper. "Surely, you ought to be satisfied. You have challenged the lion. The beast is in such awe of you that he declines the combat."

"That is true," answered Don Quixote.

"Well, then, what more can you wish? You have shown your greatness by your courage. No knight is expected to do more than challenge his enemy and wait for him on the field."

"You are right, Sir Keeper. Shut the door, and then write a little note for me, stating what you have seen me do. Shut the door as I bid you, and I will call those back who ran away for safety. They must hear your account of my exploit."

The keeper gladly obeyed, and Don Quixote waved a handkerchief from the point of his lance.

Sancho was the first to see the signal. "There, there!" he cried to the wagoner. "I'll be switched, if my master has not overcome those lions."

They waited a few moments, and then seeing everything quiet about the wagon, they went cautiously back.

"Come on, friend," said Don Quixote to the wagoner. "Hitch up your mules again, and go your way. And Sancho, open your purse and give to each of these men two gold pieces to pay them for the time they have lost."

"I'll do that with all my heart," answered Sancho. "But where are the lions? Are they dead, or alive?"

Then the keeper gave a glowing account of the combat, and told how the lion, being overawed at the very sight of Don Quixote, was utterly unable to stir from the cage.

"What do you think of that, Sancho?" said the proud knight. "Courage is even greater than enchantment."

So the two gold pieces were paid to the men; the wagoner hitched his mules to the wagon; the lions were duly fed; and the keeper, well satisfied with the day's adventure, climbed up to his seat on the front part of the cage.

"Sir, good-by," he said, doffing his hat to Don Quixote. "I thank you, and I will tell the king about your wonderful prowess."

"Do so, my friend," answered our hero; "and if the king should ask who it was that challenged the beast, tell him it was the Knight of the Lions; for that is the name by which I wish the world to know me."

The wagoner cracked his whip and shouted; the mules strained at their traces; the wagon rumbled slowly away, down the long road; and Don Quixote and Sancho Panza resumed their journey.

22. The Enchanted Bark

FAIR and softly, and step by step, did Don Quixote and his squire wend their way through field and wood and village and farmland. Many and strange were their adventures—so many and strange, indeed, that I shall not try to relate the half of them.

At length, on a sunny day, they came to the banks of the river Ebro. As the knight sat on Rozinante's back and gazed at the flowing water and at the grass and trees which bordered the banks with living green, he felt very happy. His squire, however, was in no pleasant humor; for the last few days had been days of weary toil.

Presently Don Quixote observed a little boat which was lying in the water nearby, being moored by a rope to the trunk of a small tree. It had neither oars nor sail, and for that reason it seemed all the more inviting.

The knight dismounted from his steed, calling at the same time to his squire to do the same.

"Alight, Sancho," he said. "Let us tie our beasts to the branches of this willow."

Sancho obeyed, asking, "Why do we alight here, master?"

"You are to know," answered Don Quixote, "that this boat lies here for us. It invites me to embark in it and hasten to the relief of some knight, or other person of high degree, who is in distress."

"I wonder if that is so," said Sancho.

"Certainly," answered his master. "In all the books that I have read, enchanters are forever doing such things. If a knight happens to be in danger, there is sometimes only one other knight that can rescue him. So a boat is provided for that other knight, and, in the twinkling of an eye, he is whisked away to the scene of trouble, even though it be two or three thousand leagues."

"That is wonderful," said Sancho.

"Most assuredly," answered Don Quixote; "and it is for just such a purpose that this enchanted bark lies here. Therefore let us leave our steeds here in the shade and embark in it."

"Well, well," said Sancho, "since you are the master, I must obey. But I tell you this is no enchanted bark. It is some fisherman's boat."

"They are usually fishermen's boats," said Don Quixote. "So, let us begin our voyage without delay."

He leaped into the little vessel. Sancho followed, and untied the rope. The boat drifted slowly out into the stream.

When Sancho saw that they were out of reach of the shore and had no means of pushing back, he began to quake with fear.

"We shall never see our noble steeds again," he cried. "Hear how the poor donkey brays and moans because we are leaving him. See how Rozinante tugs at his bridle. Oh, my poor, dear friends, good-by!"

Then he began such a moaning and howling that Don Quixote lost all patience with him.

"Coward!" he cried. "What are you afraid of? Who is after you? Who hurts you? Why, we have already floated some seven or eight hundred leagues. If I'm not mistaken, we shall soon pass the equinoctial line which divides the earth into two equal parts."

"And when we come to that line, how far have we gone then?" asked Sancho.

"A mighty way," answered the knight.

They were now floating down the river with some speed. Below them were two great water mills near the middle of the stream.

"Look! look, my Sancho!" cried Don Quixote. "Do you see yon city or castle? That is where some knight lies in prison, or some princess is detained against her will."

"What do you mean?" asked Sancho. "Don't you see that those are no castles? They are only water mills for grinding corn."

"Peace, Sancho! I know they look like water mills, but that is a trick of the enchanters. Why, those vile fellows can change and overturn everything from its natural form. You know how they transformed my Dulcinea."

The boat was now moving quite rapidly with the current. The people in the mills saw it and came out with long poles to keep it clear of the great water wheels. They were powdered with flour dust, as millers commonly are, and therefore looked quite uncanny.

"Hello, there!" they cried. "Are you mad, in that boat? Push off, or you'll be cut to pieces by the mill wheels."

"Didn't I tell you, Sancho, that this is the place where I must show my strength?" said Don Quixote. "See how those hobgoblins come out against us! But I'll show them what sort of person I am."

Then he stood up in the boat and began to call the millers all sorts of bad names.

"You paltry cowards!" he cried. "Release at once the captive whom you are detaining within your castle. For I am Don Quixote de la Mancha, the Knight of the Lions, whom heaven has sent to set your prisoner free."

He drew his sword and began to thrust the air with it, as though fighting with an invisible enemy. But the millers gave little heed to his actions, and stood ready with their poles to stop the boat.

Sancho threw himself on his knees in the bottom of the boat and began to pray for deliverance. And, indeed, it seemed as though their time had come, for they were drifting straight into the wheel. Quickly the millers bestirred themselves, and thrusting out their poles, they overturned the boat.

Don Quixote and Sancho were, of course, spilled out into the stream. It was lucky that both could swim. The weight of the knight's armor dragged him twice to the bottom and both he and his squire would have been drowned had not two of the millers jumped in and pulled them out by main force.

Hardly had our exhausted heroes recovered their senses when the fisherman who owned the boat came running down to the shore. When he saw that the little craft had been broken to pieces in the mill wheel, he fell upon Sancho and began to beat him unmercifully.

"You shall pay me for that boat," he cried.

129

"I am ready to pay for it," said Don Quixote, "provided these people will fairly and immediately surrender the prisoners whom they have unjustly detained in their castle."

"What castle do you mean? and what prisoners?" asked the millers. "Explain yourself, sir. We don't know what you are talking about."

"I might as well talk to a stump as try to persuade you to do a good act," answered Don Quixote. "Now, I see that two rival enchanters have clashed in this adventure. One sent me a boat, the other overwhelmed it in the river. It is very plain that I can do nothing where there is such plotting and counter-plotting."

Then he turned his face toward the mill and raised his eyes to the window above the wheel.

"My friends!" he cried at the top of his voice; "my friends, whoever you are who lie immured in that prison, hear me! Pardon my ill luck, for I cannot set you free. You must needs wait for some other knight to perform that adventure."

Having said this, he ordered Sancho to pay the fisherman fifty reals for the boat.

Sancho obeyed sullenly, for he was very unwilling to part with the money.

"Two voyages like that will sink all our stock," he muttered.

The fisherman and the millers stood with their mouths open, wondering what sort of men these were who had come so strangely into their midst. Then, concluding that they were madmen, they left them, the millers going to their mill, and the fisherman to his hut.

As for Don Quixote and Sancho, they trudged sorrowfully back to their beasts; and thus ended the adventure of the enchanted bark.

23. The Duke and the Duchess

ONE fine day, just before sunset, our travelers came suddenly into a broad, green meadow which was bordered on three sides by a wood. In this meadow they saw a company of men and women whom Don Quixote guessed to be fine people out for a hunt. Nor was he at all mistaken.

He stopped and watched them from a distance. The chief person in the company was a lady, dressed in green attire so rich that nothing could be richer. She was riding on a white horse appareled with a silver saddle and trappings of green. On her left wrist sat a hawk; and by this sign Don Quixote knew her to be the mistress of the company.

Presently, he called softly to his squire. "Friend Sancho," he said, "go quickly and tell that lady on the white palfrey that I, the Knight of the Lions, humbly salute her great beauty. But be careful what you say, and don't make a show of yourself by quoting proverbs."

"Your command shall be obeyed," said Sancho; and he at once set forward as fast as his donkey would carry him. As he drew near to the fair huntress he alighted and fell on his knees before her.

"Fair lady," he said, "yonder knight is called the Knight of the Lions, and he is my master. I am his squire, and my name is Sancho Panza. He has sent me to tell you that he has no mind but to serve your hawking beauty and—and—"

"Pray rise, good squire," said the lady. "I have heard of this Knight of the Lions, and it is not at all fitting that his squire should remain on his knees. Rise, sir, rise."

Sancho got up. He was surprised at the lady's beauty. He was also surprised to learn that she had heard of his master. He stood before her with wide-open mouth, waiting for her further commands.

"Tell me," she said, "is not your master the ingenious gentleman, Don Quixote de la Mancha?"

"The very same, may it please your worship," answered Sancho; "and that squire of his is Sancho Panza by name, my own self."

"I am very glad to hear all this," said the lady. "And I, too," said Sancho.

"Now, go, friend Panza," said the lady, "and tell your master that I am glad to welcome him to my estates. Nothing could give me more happiness."

Sancho was overjoyed. He hastened back to his master and repeated every word that had been said to him.

Don Quixote listened quietly. Then he fixed himself in his saddle, and arranged his armor. He roused up Rozinante, and set off at a good round pace to kiss the hand of the fair huntress.

By this time, the lady, who was indeed a duchess, had been joined by her husband, the duke, and both stood waiting for his coming; for they had heard of his many exploits, and they wished to become acquainted with him.

As Don Quixote rode up and was about to alight, Sancho hastened to be ready to hold his stirrup. But as he was sliding from the donkey's back his foot was caught in the pack saddle, and there he hung by the heel with head on the ground.

It was a funny sight, but everybody was looking at Don Quixote, and Sancho was left to struggle as he might.

Don Quixote, who was used to having his stirrup held, now made bold to alight without his squire's help. He came suddenly down into the stirrup with all his weight; and Rozinante's saddle girth turning, he tumbled upon the ground between the poor horse's feet.

The duke's men ran to help Don Quixote to his feet. He was not hurt much. He brushed the dust from his hands and went limping toward the spot where the duke and duchess were waiting.

The duke met him and embraced him. "I am sorry," he said, "that such a mischance should happen to you here on my territories."

"Valorous prince," said Don Quixote, "I count it no mischance when I may have the happiness of seeing your grace. My squire is much more apt to let his tongue loose than to tighten my saddle girth. But, whether I be down or up, on horseback or on foot, I am always at your command."

Then he went on to salute the duchess and to pay many a pretty compliment to her beauty and her wisdom.

The end of the whole matter was that the duke invited him to stay for a while at his castle, which was not far away.

"I entreat you, most valorous Knight of the Lions," he said, "to favor us with your company. You shall have such entertainment as is due to a person so justly famous."

Don Quixote thereupon mounted his Rozinante again, the duke got upon his own stately steed, and the duchess riding between them, they moved toward the castle, which was situated among the hills not far away.

The duchess was delighted with Sancho. He was always so ready with an excuse or a proverb that he amused her beyond measure.

"Why not let your squire ride with us?" she presently asked.

Sancho needed no further invitation. He crowded in between the duke and the duchess, and thus made a fourth rider in the notable procession that was ambling toward the duke's castle.

They were yet some little distance from the gates when the duke gave spurs to his steed and galloped on ahead. He hastened homeward to put things in readiness for his guests and to direct his people how to behave themselves toward the valorous knight, Don Quixote.

When at length the party arrived at the gate of the castle, they were met by two of the duke's servants. These servants were dressed in long vests of crimson satin, cut and shaped like nightgowns.

They went directly to Don Quixote. They took him in their arms, and lifted him from the saddle to the ground.

Then they said to him, "Go, great and mighty sir, and help our Lady Duchess down."

Don Quixote hastened to obey, but the lady objected. Many pretty compliments were passed back and forth while the fair duchess sat upon her palfrey.

"I will not alight," she said, "except in my husband's arms."

So the duke came and took her down; and Don Quixote bowed his apologies and walked by her side through the broad gateway. As they entered the courtyard they were met by two beautiful girls who threw a mantle of fine scarlet over Don Quixote's shoulders. Then all the servants of the duke, both men and women, shouted, "Welcome, welcome, flower and cream of knight-errantry!"

All these things pleased Don Quixote amazingly. For this was the first time he had felt that he was really and truly a knight. He now found himself treated just like the famous heroes he had read about, and it did his heart good.

They led him up a stately staircase and into a noble hall, all hung with rich gold brocade. There his armor was taken off by six young ladies, who served him instead of pages.

"This is, indeed, like the glorious days of chivalry," he said to himself.

But what a poor piece of humanity he was when unarmed! Raw-boned and meager, tall and lank, lantern-jawed and toothless, he was indeed an odd-looking figure. The young ladies who waited on him had much ado to stifle their laughter.

With much dignity, however, he retired to his own room, where he dressed himself for dinner. He put on his belt and sword, threw a scarlet cloak over his shoulders, and set a jaunty cap of green velvet upon his head. When he came back into the hall you would not have known him.

Twelve pages at once came forward to lead him to the dinner table. Some walked before, some followed behind, and all waited upon him with the greatest show of respect.

The table was set for four persons only, and there Don Quixote was received by the duke and the duchess and a priest who was with them. Courtly compliments were passed on all sides, and then they seated themselves, one at each of the four sides of the table.

Now the reason for all the kindness shown to Don Quixote was this: The duke and duchess had nothing to do but to pass away the time, and they had found this to be the very hardest kind of work. They had become tired of hunting, tired of playing chess, tired of watching the servants at work, tired of music, tired of everything.

"Oh, life is so dull and wearisome!" they said to each other. "Can't something be done to make it more enjoyable?"

So, when Don Quixote and his squire happened to come to them, they were overjoyed. "We shall have great sport with this rare couple," said the duke. "We shall have something to laugh at for the rest of our lives."

The duchess agreed to all his plans, and Don Quixote was therefore invited to make his home in the castle. He would give them more amusement than any fool at the king's court. And every day of his stay with them, the duke and the duchess studied how they might invent some new and pleasant joke upon the knight or his squire. Everything was done kindly so as to hurt no one's feelings; and so many tricks were played that it would take more pages than there are in this book to tell about them all.

I will relate only one or two.

24. The Wooden-Peg Horse

ONE evening the duke and the duchess were amusing themselves by listening to Don Quixote's valorous talk.

"Do you know of any case of injured innocence?" he asked. "I will avenge it. I will go to the ends of the earth to combat error. I am not afraid of giants nor even of enchanters. I will fight them, one and all, in defense of truth."

While he was thus boasting of his valor there was a sound of fifes and drums, and twelve elderly women entered, all clad in the dress of nuns. After them came a noble lady, heavily veiled and wearing a gown with a long trail divided into three parts.

The twelve women ranged themselves in two rows, and thus made a lane for the strange lady to march through as she approached the duke and duchess. Then her squire, who followed her, announced that she was the Countess Trifaldin, otherwise known as the Disconsolate Lady, and that she had come from a distant land to make known her misfortunes.

The duke received her graciously. He took her by the hand and placed her in a chair by the side of the duchess. Don Quixote and Sancho stood anxiously near, both wishing very much to see the veiled lady's face.

After the usual compliments had been passed, the lady suddenly asked, "Is there in this illustrious company a knight called Don Quixote de la Manchissima with his squirissimo Panza?"

"Panza is here," cried Sancho, before anybody else could speak; "and here is Don Quixotissimo also. So you may tell your tale, fair lady, for we are all ready to be your servitorissimos."

Then Don Quixote spoke. "I am the valorous Don Quixote de la Mancha," he said. "My profession is to succor the distressed, and I therefore dedicate my service to you. Tell us of your troubles, madam, and if they do not admit of a cure, we can at least sympathize with you."

The veiled lady, with sighs and sobs and many high-sounding words, at length related her story.

She declared that she had come from the distant kingdom of Candaya, where she had once ranked among the noblest of the land. A giant wizard named Malambruno had bewitched her and placed her under a spell of enchantment.

138

Until that spell could be removed she was doomed to wander over the earth in search of a champion who would restore her to her rightful place and honors.

"Ah, madam!" cried Don Quixote, "behold in me your champion. Point out the way, and I will go to the ends of the earth to serve you."

Then the lady told him that the kingdom of Candaya was thousands of leagues away, and that to travel thither by any ordinary means would require many years.

"But the wizard Malambruno will send you a steed," said she; "he will send you a magic steed that will carry you to Candaya quickly and with the greatest ease. For he has heard of your prowess, and he is anxious to test it by meeting you in mortal combat."

"Pray tell me, of what nature is that steed which he will send for my conveyance?" said Don Quixote.

"It is the steed Clavileño," answered the lady—"the same wooden horse, in fact, which the wizard Merlin lent to his friend Peter of Provence. It is indeed a wondrous steed. It never eats nor sleeps nor needs shoeing. It has no wings, and yet it goes ambling through the air, so smoothly that you may carry a cup of water in your hand and not spill a drop of it. If you are bold enough to ride this horse, and—"

"Bold enough!" interrupted Don Quixote. "Who questions my boldness? Bring the steed to me, and you shall see that I shrink from nothing."

"The steed shall be ready for you in the morning," answered the lady.

Early the next day, therefore, the duke, with his household and guests, went into the garden to see the outcome of this adventure. They were all greatly delighted, for the whole matter had been arranged on purpose for their amusement.

Don Quixote soon arrived. He was clad in his armor, with his sword dangling from his side, and he seemed very impatient of delay. Sancho was close at his heels, but by no means pleased with the undertaking.

About the middle of the forenoon a trumpet sounded and four woodsmen came into the garden. They were dressed in green, with wreaths of ivy about their heads. They carried between them a misshapen, long-legged wooden horse, which they set down upon the ground.

"Here is the famous Clavileño," cried their leader. "There is none like him upon the earth. Now let the man who is not afraid mount him, and away at once for Candaya. And let his squire, if he has one, mount behind him; for the steed flies best when fully weighted."

"But I see no bridle," said Sancho. "How is the noble beast to be guided?"

"Simply by turning this wooden peg which you see in his forehead," answered the woodsman. "It is very easy to direct him either to the right or to the left. But the knight and his squire must both be blindfolded; otherwise they become giddy in their flight through the upper air and tumble headlong to the earth."

Don Quixote did not hesitate a moment. He climbed into the saddle. He pulled a handkerchief from his pocket and asked one of the ladies to hoodwink him with it. Then he noticed that Sancho hung back and seemed afraid.

"What! you rascal!" he cried. "Are you afraid to sit where many better than you have sat? Come, suffer yourself to be blindfolded, and let me not hear a word of complaint from you."

Soon both knight and squire were astride of the steed and blindfolded. They were ready to begin their perilous flight.

The duke and the duchess and all their household came around and bade them good-by. Then Don Quixote leaned forward and began to turn the pin in the horse's head. He fancied that he was rising in the air, and that he was sailing right up to the sky.

"Speed you well, brave knight!" cried all the people in the garden. "May Heaven be your guide, bold squire!"

Then they clapped their hands, and shouted: "How high you are! How like a blazing star you shoot through the sky. Hold fast, Sancho! Don't loosen your hold and fall from that giddy height."

"Sir," said Sancho, clinging close to his master "how does it happen that we can hear them so plainly although we are soaring so high above them? One would think that they were standing close beside us."

"It is all very natural," answered Don Quixote; "for in these grand aerial flights you can see and hear things plainly which are a thousand leagues away. But don't hold me so hard; you will make me tumble off."

"I wish only to steady you," said Sancho.

"Well, I wonder what makes you tremble so," said Don Quixote. "As for myself, I never rode easier in my life. The horse goes as if he were not moving at all."

After a few minutes, he said, "I think that we must now be somewhere in the second region of the air, where hail and snow are produced. If we keep on at this rate we shall soon reach the third region, from which the lightnings and the thunderbolts are hurled upon the earth. I hope that we shall not go too near the sun, for in that case we shall surely be scorched."

At that moment one of the duke's men set fire to some flax at the end of a pole and swished it near their faces.

"Well! well!" cried Sancho. "We are in the region of fire already; for the half of my beard is singed off. I have a great mind to peep out under the blindfold and see what sort of country we are coming to."

"Don't do it, for—your life," said Don Quixote. "The whole issue of this adventure depends upon obedience. Be brave, be patient; for we only mount high in order that we may come straight down upon the kingdom of Candaya."

"Shall we be there soon, master?" asked Sancho.

"I know not," was the answer; "but we have certainly already traversed a vast distance."

"Well, I should like it better if I had a softer saddle," said Sancho.

The duke and duchess were mightily pleased at the success of their joke. The question now was how they could put a fitting end to the well-contrived adventure.

One of the servants ran up and set fire to Clavileño's tail. The horse, being filled with fireworks, burst open with a tremendous noise. Don Quixote and his squire were, of course, thrown to the ground. They were scorched a little, but not otherwise hurt.

They scrambled to their feet and pulled the bandages from their eyes. They looked around, and were surprised to find themselves still in the duke's garden, where they had begun their flight. As they recovered from their confusion, they saw a lance sticking in the ground nearby, and on the lance was a scroll of white parchment bound around with two green ribbons.

Don Quixote looked at the scroll, and seeing his name upon it, picked it off to read what was written. The inscription was in golden characters, and read as follows:—

"The renowned knight, Don Quixote, has achieved this adventure by honestly trying to perform it. Malambruno is fully satisfied. The enchantment is removed from all who have suffered by it. This is ordered by

"MERLIN, Prince of enchanters."

"What wonderful fortune is ours!" cried Don Quixote, after reading it. "Let us have courage, for the adventure is finished, and we have accomplished everything without damage to anybody."

And now the duke came forward and greeted him as the bravest knight the world had ever seen. The duchess, her face wreathed with smiles, shook hands with both knight and squire.

"How did you fare on your long and perilous journey?" she asked.

"Very pleasantly, madam," answered Sancho. "I never had so wonderful a view of creation in my life. For, as we were flying through the region of fire, I shoved my handkerchief over a little and peeped down. Ah! it was a sight to gladden the eyes. I spied the earth, far, far below us, and it looked no bigger than a mustard seed."

"Indeed, it must have been very wonderful," said the duchess.

"It was nothing short of wonderful," said Sancho. "Why, I could see the men walking about on the earth, and I declare they looked no bigger than hazelnuts."

The duchess laughed. "Men the size of hazelnuts walking on an earth the size of a mustard seed!" she said. "It must have been very, very, wonderful."

"Truly it was," answered Sancho. "And at one time when I looked between my eyelashes, I saw myself so near to heaven that I could almost reach out and touch it. Then we passed the place where the seven stars are, and I saw seven frisky goats in a great pasture. What did I do but slip off of Clavileño without telling a soul? And there I played and leaped with the goats for fully three quarters of an hour."

"And what became of your master and the horse while you were playing?" asked the duchess.

Sancho scratched his head and was at a loss for an answer.

"Well, madam, I— I—" he stammered. "Well, I—"

"Speak out," said the duke. "Say that the noble steed stirred not a foot, but waited patiently about till the game was over."

"'Truly, he did that very thing," said Sancho.

The duke and his servants laughed heartily, but they were not quite sure whether Sancho was in earnest or otherwise. What if, after all, he had seen through their cunning little play, and was now slyly making game of them?

Don Quixote said but little; and yet he looked and acted as though he were very proud and well satisfied with the result of his achievement.

And so ended the famous adventure with the wooden-peg horse.

25. Sancho on His Island

THE duke and the duchess were so well pleased with the success of their latest jest that they soon formed plans for another; and this time Sancho Panza was to be the chosen hero.

"Sancho Panza," said the duke one day, "is it true that your master has promised to make you the governor of an island?"

"Aye, so he has," answered Sancho; "and I am he that deserves it as well as anybody. I have kept my master company many a month; and if he live and I live, there will be no lack of islands for me to govern."

"Well," said the duke, "I have a few spare islands of my own lying around, and I will give you one for the sake of my good friend Don Quixote."

"Down, down on thy knees, Sancho," cried Don Quixote, "and kiss the duke's feet for this favor."

And Sancho obeyed.

A few days later the duke said to the squire, "Sancho, do you remember the island which I promised you?"

"Most assuredly, sir, I have not forgotten it," said Sancho.

"Well, you must prepare to take possession of your government to-morrow," said the duke. "The islanders are longing for you as a farmer longs for rain in summer. They will not be put off any longer."

Sancho bowed humbly and answered, "Well then, I will do my best. But since I looked down from the sky the other day and saw the earth so very small, I don't care half so much about being governor. What does it matter to rule over half-a-dozen men no bigger than hazelnuts?"

"Oh, Sancho," said the duke, "when once you have had a taste of ruling you will never leave off licking your fingers, you will find it so sweet to command and so pleasant to be obeyed."

"Indeed it is a dainty thing to command," said Sancho. "I know it, for I once commanded a flock of sheep."

"Well, I hope you will be as good a governor as you were a shepherd," said the duke. "Now get ready to set out for your island to-morrow morning. My servants will furnish you with dress suitable to your high office."

"Let them dress me as they will, I'll be Sancho Panza still," answered the squire.

When Don Quixote heard that Sancho was to leave for his island in the morning he sat down with him and gave him a great deal of good advice. Among a thousand other things, he said:—

"First of all, fear God; for the fear of Him is wisdom.

"Secondly, make it thy business to know thyself.

"Pride thyself more on being humble and virtuous than proud and vicious.

"Despise not thy poor relations.

"Let the tears of the poor find more compassion than the testimony of the rich.

"Revile not with words him whom thou hast to punish in deed.

"In the trial of a criminal remember the temptations of our depraved nature, and show thyself full of pity and mercy.

"As to the government of thy person, my first command is cleanliness.

"Pare thy nails.

"Keep thy clothes well-fitted about thee.

"Defile not thy breath with onions and garlic.

"Walk softly, speak with deliberation.

"Drink moderately.

"Be careful not to chew on both sides.

"Sleep with moderation.

"As for thy dress, wear long hose, an ample coat, and a cloak a little larger.

"Lastly, do not overlard thy discourse with proverbs, as thou art wont to do."

Sancho listened quietly to all this advice and promised that he would observe as much of it as he could remember.

"But please let me have it all in black and white," he said; "for my memory is poor. True, I can neither write nor read, but I will give it to the priest of my island and tell him to hammer it into me as often as I need it."

"Oh, sinner that I am!" cried Don Quixote. "How scandalous it is that a governor should not be able to read or write! I would have thee at least learn to write thy name."

"Oh, I can write my name." answered Sancho. "I used to scrawl a sort of letters, and they told me it was my name. Besides, I can pretend that I've hurt my hand, and get somebody else to sign for me. For there is a remedy for all things but death. Let them backbite me to my face, I will bite-back the biters. Let them come for wool and go home shorn. The rich man's follies pass for wise sayings. What a man has, so much is he worth, said my grandmother."

"Enough! enough!" said Don Quixote. "We have had enough of your proverbs. They will make your islanders plot against you and pull you down."

"For pity's sake, master!" said Sancho, "don't grudge me the use of my own goods. Proverbs are all my stock. Whether the pitcher hit the stone, or the stone hit the pitcher, it is bad for the pitcher."

"Well, Sancho," answered Don Quixote, "you have a good disposition, and you mean well. So let us go to dinner."

The very next day Sancho set out for his island. He was dressed in fine clothes, and rode a tall mule in gaudy trappings. Behind him was led his own donkey, adorned like a horse of state.

He kissed the hands of the duke and duchess, and bowed his head to receive his master's blessing. Then he rode tearfully away with a great train of servants, every one of whom had been told how to behave towards him.

It was not a long journey. Soon they came to a little town which belonged to the duke, and Sancho was told that it was his island. Its name was Barataria.

At the gates of the town he was met by the chief officers. The bells rang, and the people shouted their joy. Then he was led to the church, and the keys of the town were put in his hands.

"Hail to our noble governor!" shouted young and old; and Sancho began to feel very much elated.

He was so short and fat, and he looked so funny in his fine clothes, that all who did not know that it was one of the duke's jokes were puzzled to think what kind of man he was. But still they shouted, "Hail to our lord, Don Sancho Panza!"

Sancho turned to his secretary and asked, "Whom do they call Don Sancho Panza?"

"Why, your lordship, yourself," answered the secretary.

"Well, friend," said Sancho, "take notice that Don does not belong to me. Plain Sancho Panza is my name. My father and my grandfather and all of us have been plain Panzas without Dons or Donnas added. Now, I guess the Dons are as thick as stones on this island, but if my government lasts four days I'll clear them out, like so many flies."

From the church Sancho was taken with much ceremony to the Hall of Justice. There he was set in a great chair, and all who wished to appeal to him for justice came and made their wants known.

The first who came were two men, one dressed like a country fellow, the other like a tailor.

"My lord governor," said the tailor, "this farmer and I have come for you to settle a dispute between us. Yesterday the farmer came into my shop with a piece of cloth. He asked me if there was enough of it to make a cap. I measured the stuff and answered, Yes. Then he asked if there was enough for two caps, and I

147

again said, Yes. At last, I told him there was enough for five caps. This morning he came for his caps. They were finished and I gave them to him. But he would not pay me. He says I must give him his cloth again, or the price of it."

Sancho turned to the farmer and said, "Is this true, my friend?"

"Yes," answered the man, "but let him show you the five caps he has made."

"With all my heart," said the tailor; and with that he held up his hand, showing four tiny caps on his fingers and one on his thumb.

"There," said he, "you see the five caps he asked for, and I have not a snip of cloth left."

Everybody in the room laughed to see the number of caps and their smallness.

Sancho put his hand to his chin and thought for a little while. Then he said, "It is the judgment of this court that the tailor shall lose his making, and the farmer his cloth. The caps shall be given to the prisoners in jail; and that ends the whole matter."

All who heard this decision were pleased because of its justice.

Two old men next came before the governor. One of them carried a cane, which he used to help him along.

"My lord," said the other man, "some time ago I lent this good man ten gold crowns. I did it as an act of kindness, and he was to repay me whenever I asked him. I did not demand it for a long time; but since he seemed so careless about it, I at last said to him that I wanted the money. What do you think? He not only refuses to pay me, but he says I never lent him the money, or if I did, he returned it. I have no witnesses, but I beg you to put him on his oath. If he will swear that he has paid me, I will forgive him."

"Old man of the staff," said Sancho, "what say you to this?"

"Sir," answered the old man, "I own that he lent me the money. And if you will hold out your rod of office, I will swear upon it that I have returned it in full."

Sancho held out the rod. The old man handed his staff to the other man to hold while he took the oath. Then he put his hands on the cross of the governor's rod, and swore that it was true that the other had lent him the money, but that he had returned the same sum into his hands.

Sancho turned to the other man and asked, "What do you say to that?"

"Well," said the poor man, "my neighbor is a good Christian, and I don't believe he would swear falsely. Perhaps I have forgotten when and how he repaid me."

Then the owner of the staff took his stick, and the two men left the court.

Sancho leaned his head over his breast, he put his forefinger on his eyebrows, and sat silent for a time. Then he suddenly said:—

"Where is that man with the staff? Bring him back to me instantly."

Soon both men were again brought before him.

"Good man," said he to the one with the staff, "let me see your cane. I have use for it."

"Certainly, sir. Here it is," answered the man. Sancho took the staff and immediately gave it to the other man.

"There," he said, "go your way in peace, for now you are paid."

"How so, my lord?" cried the man. "Is this cane worth ten gold crowns?"

"Well, if it is not, then I am the greatest fool in the world," said Sancho. "If you will but return the cane to me for a moment, you shall see with your own eyes."

He took the staff between his hands and broke it in two; and out fell the ten gold crowns.

Everybody in the court was amazed. They began to think that Sancho was a second Solomon, whose wisdom was past finding out. The truth was, however, that Sancho had once heard of the same kind of trick being played in a distant town. It was an old story, but unknown in Barataria.

The end of the matter was that one old man went away very much ashamed, and the other returned home well satisfied.

Thus, one case after another was brought before the "governor," and he gave such wise judgment that the people wondered how such wisdom could be contained in a little round head like his. And yet, with all the attention that was shown him, Sancho was not happy in his island.

He was never allowed to eat a good meal; for the doctor always stood by and refused to let him touch anything that would hurt his digestion. He could not even eat roast partridge, although it was set on the table before him, and was of all things the dish which he liked best.

He was wearied, too, with all the tedious ceremonies at court. His fine clothes were irksome. His night's sleep was broken into by the cares of state. And then, at last, there came a dreadful letter from the duke.

The letter was full of warnings. Some enemies, it said, were marching against the island. Four men had gone to the town for the purpose of killing the governor. The duke therefore advised Sancho to be careful, and not eat anything that was set before him, lest he should be poisoned.

All this was a part of the duke's great joke, and it frightened Sancho Panza terribly.

Seven days had passed since he came to Barataria. He had had no rest. He was tired and hungry. It was very late when he was at last allowed to go to bed.

He was just dropping off to sleep when he heard a great noise in the street. He was alarmed and jumped up to see what was the matter.

Bells were ringing, drums were beating, men were shouting. Sancho trembled with fear. He put on his slippers, and hurried to the door.

150

Several men with torches and drawn swords came running up. They shouted:—

"Arm, arm, Lord Governor! The enemy have got into the island. Come and lead us against them. We have arms for you!"

"Why, then arm me, and good luck to us all," said Sancho, trying to be very brave.

They brought two shields and put them over his shirt, one behind and one before. They fastened these shields together with cords drawn as tightly as possible. Then they put a spear in his hand and said, "Lead on, now, Lord Governor!"

"How can I lead on, when I am trussed up like this?" asked Sancho; and indeed he looked much like a turtle between two great shells.

"I cannot so much as bend my legs," said he. "You must carry me."

"Nonsense, my Lord Governor," said one of the men. "It is fear that keeps you from moving. Lead on, for the danger is greater every minute."

Poor Sancho tried to walk; but he fell to the floor with such a crash that he thought himself broken to pieces. He lay there, helpless and praying for deliverance.

Suddenly all the lights went out. He could hear men fighting all around. Some tripped on him. Some stood on him and shouted. He was never so frightened in his life.

"Oh, that this island were taken," he moaned, "or that I were dead and out of this trouble."

Then he heard shouts of "Victory! victory! Where is our lord governor?"

Sancho could only cry in a weak voice, "Here I am. Help me up!"

His shields were taken off, and he was carried into his chamber. There he fell back on his bed in a dead swoon, and those who had been playing this joke upon him became really frightened.

By and by, however, he began to come to himself.

"What time is it?" he asked.

"It is near daybreak," they answered.

He spoke not again, but very quietly began to put on his clothes.

When he was dressed he went out slowly and feebly, for he was too much bruised to move fast. He went to the stable and found the stall where his donkey was standing.

He flung his arms around the beast's neck and kissed him.

"Oh, my dear Dapple!" he said, while tears fell from his eyes. "My faithful companion, my best friend! When all my cares were only to feed thy little body, my hours, my days, my years were happy. But since I clambered up upon the tower of ambition, I have a thousand woes, a thousand toils, and four thousand tribulations."

While he was talking he bridled and saddled the donkey. Then he slowly got upon him and took hold of the reins.

153

"Make way, gentlemen!" he cried to those who were standing around. "Let me return to liberty. I was not born to be a governor, or to defend islands. May heaven bless you, my good people! Tell my lord duke that I have neither won nor lost; for I came into this island without a penny, and without a penny I leave it. Clear the way, then, and let me go!"

So saying, he chirruped to his donkey and rode slowly away to rejoin his master, Don Quixote.

Everybody appeared to be astonished when he finally arrived at the duke's castle. Yet all welcomed him kindly and heartily, and listened to his story of what had happened to him.

"It is now eight days since I began to govern the island that was given me," he said. "In all that time I never had enough to eat. I had no leisure either to take bribes or to receive what were my just dues. Enemies trampled over my bones. My life was a burden. But man proposes, and God disposes. Heaven knows what is best for us all. Let no man say, I will not drink of this water. I say no more."

"Never mind, Sancho, never mind," said Don Quixote. "If a governor returns rich from his government, they say he has robbed. If he returns poor, then they call him a do-little. But if thy conscience is clear, thou hast nothing to fear."

"Yes," said Sancho, "but this time they will be likelier to call me an idiot than a robber."

26. The Innkeeper of Saragossa

ONE morning towards the end of summer Don Quixote surprised the duke by calling for his armor and his steed.

"My Lord Duke, I must away, to seek new adventures," he said. "I cannot tarry here any longer."

"But has not your stay with us been agreeable to you?" asked the duke. "Why should you wish to leave us?"

"You have indeed been kind, and I thank you for it," answered the knight. "But it is wrong to linger here among the dainties and delights which you have provided, while there are so many things in the world that need doing. I shall have to give an account for all these idle days."

So, bidding the duke and duchess a kind farewell, he mounted his steed and rode away towards Saragossa; and Sancho, on his dappled donkey, followed him as before.

Time would fail me to tell of the many happenings on the road. They traveled leisurely along, making no plans, and letting each day and hour take care of itself. Yet the knight was ever on the alert for some new adventure.

One evening they arrived at an inn on the outskirts of the city, feeling very tired and hungry. The innkeeper met them at the door.

"Have you lodgings for two weary travelers and their beasts?" asked Sancho.

"Yes," answered the innkeeper, "there are no better lodgings in Saragossa."

So they alighted. Sancho led the beasts to the stable and gave them their food. Then he returned to the house to wait on his master.

"What have you for supper, my good host?" he asked.

"You may measure your mouth and ask for anything you like," said the innkeeper. "Here you will find everything in abundance—fowls of the air, birds of the earth, and fishes of the sea."

"Well," said Sancho, "if you will roast a couple of chickens for us it will be enough. My master eats but little, and I am not a glutton."

"I am sorry," said the innkeeper, "but I have not a single chicken left. The hawks have carried them all away."

"Why, then, if that is the case, you may roast us a duck," said Sancho.

"A duck, sir!" cried the innkeeper, "I sent fifty to the market yesterday, and there is not another one. But, aside from ducks and chickens, ask for anything you like."

"Well," said Sancho, "a little veal or boiled kid would taste quite good."

"Next week, my friend, we shall have plenty of both," said the host, "but now we are just out of such meats."

"Bring on some fried eggs and bacon, then," said Sancho.

"You are a good one at guessing," cried the host. "But I told you that I had neither chickens nor ducks, and so how can I have eggs?"

"Oh, bother!" said Sancho, losing his patience. "Have done with your ramblings, Mr. Landlord, and tell me just what you have."

"I will do so," answered the innkeeper. "What I really have is nothing more nor less than a pair of cow heels, dressed with beans, onions, and bacon; and all these are cooked to a turn and even now crying, 'Eat me, eat me!' "

"I set my mark on them this minute," said Sancho. "Let nobody else touch them."

"Nobody else will wish to touch them," said the inn-keeper; "for all the other guests are of such quality that they take their cook and their larder with them."

"As for quality," cried Sancho, "my master is as good as the best, but his profession doesn't allow him to carry a pantry wherever he goes."

Presently the host brought in the kettle, and they all sat down to a supper of cow's heel and onions.

The knight and his squire were used to rough fare, and they had learned to take things as they found them. They rested well that night, and in the morning set forth again upon their travels. But now, instead of going into Saragossa, they took another road and journeyed on to Barcelona.

The fame of Don Quixote had gone before him, and at Barcelona there were those who gladly received him and entertained him. And so they spent somedays in that great city, looking at its wonders and most of all at the sea which neither of them had ever before beheld.

27. The Knight of the White Moon

ONE morning Don Quixote, fully armed, rode out to the seashore to take the air. He felt very brave, and was in fine fighting humor.

"Arms," he said, "are my best attire, and combat is my meat and drink."

Suddenly he saw a strange knight riding towards him. The knight was armed from head to foot, and on his shield a bright moon was painted.

As soon as he was within hearing, he called out: "Most illustrious, most valorous Don Quixote, de la Mancha, I am the Knight of the White Moon. I have come to enter into combat with thee. I have come to make thee confess that my lady, whoever she may be, is more beautiful by far than thy Dulcinea del Toboso."

"That I will never confess," answered Don Quixote; "but I will force thee to confess the contrary. Thou hast never seen the illustrious Dulcinea. If thou hadst, the sight of her would have made thee know that there is no beauty like unto hers."

"I challenge you to prove it in fair combat," cried the Knight of the White Moon. "If I vanquish you, I shall require of you to go to your home, and for the space of one year give up your arms and your knight-errantry and live there in peace and quiet."

"But what do you agree to do if I shall vanquish you?" said Don Quixote.

"I agree that my head shall be at your disposal," answered the knight. "My horse and arms shall be your spoils, and the fame of my deeds shall be added to that of your own achievements."

"I accept your challenge," said Don Quixote; "and will faithfully comply with all its conditions; but I am content with the fame of my own deeds, and do not wish to assume yours. Choose whichever side of the field you prefer, and let us settle this business at once."

The two knights turned their horses and rode apart some distance. Then they again faced each other. The next moment, without waiting for any signal, they made the onset.

The White Moon's steed was much swifter than Rozinante, and he thundered down upon Don Quixote ere he had run one third of the distance. Our knight had no time to use his spear. The stranger struck him with such force that both he and his steed were hurled helpless to the ground.

Quickly the White Moon dismounted. He held his spear at Don Quixote's throat and cried: "Yield, knight! Fulfill the conditions of our challenge or your life is forfeit!"

Don Quixote was bruised and stunned. But he answered in a faint and feeble voice, "I maintain that Dulcinea del Toboso is the most beautiful lady in the world, and I am the most unfortunate knight. Press on thy spear, and rid me of life."

"That I will not do," said he of the White Moon. "I will not dispute the fame of the beautiful Dulcinea. I shall be satisfied if the great Don Quixote will only return to his home for a year as was agreed to in our challenge."

"Very well," answered Don Quixote. "Since you require nothing that will tarnish the fame of the Lady Dulcinea, I will do all the rest as you desire."

They lifted Don Quixote from the ground and uncovered his face. He was very pale and weak. Rozinante still lay in the sand unable to rise. As for Sancho Panza, he was so sad and dismayed that he did not know what to do.

The Knight of the White Moon galloped away toward the city, and some of those who had seen the combat followed him. They asked him who he was, and why he had dealt so roughly with the famous but harmless Don Quixote.

"My name is Samson Carrasco," said the knight, "and I am a friend and near neighbor of Don Quixote. All that I wished in this combat was not to harm my friend, but to make him promise to return home. I think that if he can be induced to rest there quietly for a year, this madness about knight-errantry will be cured."

It was, indeed, Samson Carrasco, the same who once before, as the Knight of the Mirrors, had tried to cure his friend of his folly but had failed.

28. The Last Adventure of All

FOR six days Don Quixote lay in bed, sullen and sorrowful because of his overthrow. And all this time Sancho Panza sat beside him and tried to comfort him.

"My master," he said, "pluck up your head and be of good cheer if you can. Let us go home and quit seeking adventures in lands and places we do not know. And if you will only think, I am the one who loses most, though it is you that are in the worst pickle."

The squire's cheerful words gave fresh hope to the knight. Gradually his courage came back to him, and at length the two bade good-by to Barcelona and started for home. Don Quixote rode on Rozinante. He was unarmed and clad in a traveling coat. Sancho followed him on foot, leading his donkey, which was laden with Don Quixote's armor.

"I should not have been defeated had it not been for Rozinante's weakness," said the knight.

They traveled for many days with their faces turned steadfastly towards La Mancha. But their steeds made slow progress and they stopped often by the way.

At length they got to the top of a hill from which they could see their own peaceful little village lying in the green valley below. At this sight Sancho fell upon his knees and cried out:—

"O thou long-wished-for village, open thy eyes and behold thy child, Sancho Panza. He has come back to thee again, not very rich, yet very well flogged. O village, open thy arms, and receive also thy son, Don Quixote. While he has been vanquished by others, he has gained the victory over himself—and that is the best of all victories."

"Hush your prattle," said Don Quixote, "and let us put our best foot foremost to enter our village."

So they went down the hill, and were soon met by their old friends, the curate and the barber and faithful Samson Carrasco. Don Quixote alighted and embraced them all quite lovingly.

"I have returned home for a year," he said; "and I have a mind to turn shepherd and enjoy the solitude of the fields. If you have not much to do, I shall be pleased to have you for my companions."

They answered him pleasantly, and then, surrounded by a troop of boys, they made their way to Don Quixote's house.

The housekeeper and the niece were at the door to welcome the wanderer.

"My dear niece," he said, "I have come home for a little while. I think that I shall soon leave you again, to live the simple life of a shepherd. But help me to bed, now, for it seems to me that I am not very well."

They led him in, and made him as comfortable as they could. They cared most lovingly for him day and night. But all the strength seemed to have gone from his poor body.

The curate, the barber, and Samson Carrasco came often to see him. His good squire, Sancho Panza, sat all the time by his bedside. But in spite of every care he steadily grew more feeble.

On the sixth day the doctor told him that he was in danger and might not live long. Don Quixote asked them to leave him alone a little while, for he thought that he could sleep.

They went out of the room. He soon fell into a deep slumber, and he lay so still, with such a look of peace upon his face, that they thought he would never wake in this world.

At the end of six hours, however, he opened his eyes, and cried out: "Blessed be Almighty God, who has done me so much good. His mercies are without end."

Then they saw that his madness had left and that his mind was clear and bright.

"Send for my good friends, the curate and the barber and Samson Carrasco," he said; "for I am at the point of death, and I would make my will."

But these gentlemen had all the time been waiting at the door, and now they entered the room. Don Quixote was overjoyed to see them. "Welcome, kind friends!" he said. "I am no longer Don Quixote de la Mancha, but plain Alonzo Quixana, whom our townspeople used to call The Good. My mind is clear now, and I see the great folly that I was led into through the reading of foolish books. All those vulgar stories of knights and magicians are hateful to me, and I abhor them. But now send for my lawyer, that he may draw up my will, for my hours are numbered."

They looked at one another, wondering, and Samson Carrasco went to fetch the lawyer. The sick man roused himself and his face brightened when the man of law came and sat down by his bedside.

The will was drawn up in due form. It provided that a small sum of money should be paid to Sancho Panza for his good services, and that all the rest of the estate should go to the niece. It was signed by Alonzo Quixana, and witnessed by the curate and the barber.

Then the sick man fell back in his bed, and lay for three days without knowing anything at all. In the afternoon of the third day he fell into a gentle sleep from which he never awoke.

So ended the adventures of as good a man and as brave as Spain has ever seen.

CPSIA information can be obtained at www.ICGtesting.com
Printed in the USA
BVOW06s1839050916

461187BV00028B/248/P